The Book of Experiments

Have you ever longed to go on a voyage
of discovery?
Believe it or not, the most exciting
adventures can take place —
in your own home!

Some most amazing scientific experiments
can be performed with simple, everyday
things found in almost every household.
Experiments with air, sound, heat,
water, light — 150 adventures within
the covers of this book.

3 bcd

Leonard de Vries

THE BOOK
OF EXPERIMENTS

Translated by Eric G. Breeze

Illustrated by Joost van de Woestijne

CAROUSEL BOOKS
A DIVISION OF TRANSWORLD PUBLISHERS LTD

THE BOOK OF EXPERIMENTS
A CAROUSEL BOOK 0 552 54020 X

Originally published in Great Britain
by John Murray (Publishers) Ltd.

PRINTING HISTORY
John Murray edition published 1958
Carousel edition published 1972
Carousel edition reprinted 1972
Carousel edition reprinted 1974
Carousel edition reprinted 1976

Carousel Books are published by
Transworld Publishers Ltd., Century House,
61–63 Uxbridge Road, Ealing, London W.5.

Made and printed in Great Britain by
C. Nicholls & Company Ltd.

CONTENTS

6

Dear Reader,

Have you ever longed to go on a voyage of discovery? If so, are you disappointed that your wish has not yet come true? Let me cheer you up by showing you that everyday life can be a voyage of discovery full of surprises and adventures for anyone who enjoys the wonders of nature. Whoever wants to enjoy scientific adventures can do it... in his own home!

Believe it or not, some most amazing scientific experiments can be performed with simple, everyday things that can be found in almost every household. With their aid you can make a journey of exploration through the wonderful realm of science. I invite you most cordially to come on this journey. And not only you, but the members of your household as well - your father and mother, your relations and friends.

I shall act only as the guide; you will have to make the discoveries yourself in the form of physics and chemistry experiments. For many, many evenings you will be able to amuse yourselves. But not only shall we perform exciting experiments, we shall also attempt to find out the "how" and the "why" of the different phenomena.

Are you ready to set out? Well then, let us start on this absorbing voyage of discovery.

Leonard de Vries

Experiments with air

In 1654 Otto von Guericke astonished his countrymen with an experiment which soon became world-famous. Two hemispheres—now known as the Magdeburg hemispheres, after the town where he did it—were placed together and the air was pumped out. Sixteen horses could not pull them apart!

It is always and everywhere around us. And yet we cannot see it. What is it?

AIR! What is air?

Air is a mixture of gases: oxygen (about 21%), nitrogen (78%), and the inert gases argon, neon, helium, krypton and xenon (1%).

Moreover, air contains small amounts of hydrogen, methane, carbon dioxide and water vapour.

Has air got weight?

Yes: a cubic foot of air weighs about $1\frac{1}{3}$ oz. A room 15 ft square and 9 ft high contains about 170 lb of air.

The weight of all the air on the earth is 11,000,000,000,000,000,000 lb!

The smallest particles of the gases which make the mixture we call the air are the molecules. A molecule is smaller than a 25-millionth of an inch.

A cubic inch of air contains 420,000,000,000,000, 000,000,000 molecules. These molecules move very rapidly amongst each other; their average speed is 550 yards a second (1130 m.p.h.). Each molecule collides with other molecules 50,000,000,000 times a second.

(These figures are for air at normal temperature and pressure.)

What is air pressure?

The force that the air exerts upon everything.

By pressure we mean the force with which the air presses against one square inch of a wall.

The unit of pressure is the *atmosphere*: that is a pressure of about 14½ lb per square inch, which means a force of 14½ lb on every square inch. At sea-level the average pressure is one atmosphere.

The human body has a surface area of more than a square yard (1,296 sq.ins.). So the air presses on the body with a total force of more than 18,800 pounds!

The whole earth is surrounded by a layer of air. The density is greatest at the earth's surface. Half of all the air is found below a height of 3½ miles, and about 95% below 12½ miles. Yet as high as 625 miles above the earth there is still extremely rarefied air. All this air presses on us; we find ourselves at the bottom of an ocean of air!

1. May I pour you a glass of air?

You will need: basin of water, 2 glasses.

Pour out a glass of air! How can that be done?

Quite simply. Lay a glass in the bowl of water so that it fills with water completely. Then raise the glass, upside down, taking care that the mouth stays under the water. The glass then remains full of water. This is because of the pressure of the air of 14½ lb per square inch on the surface of the water. The pressure forces the water up inside the glass, and is actually capable of supporting a column of water 33 feet high.

Now push the second glass, B, into the water with the opening downwards. No water enters because it is found that the air in the glass B has a greater pressure than the air outside. Now tilt glass B under glass A, and the air out of B rises as bubbles into A. So glass A fills with air and B fills with water. You have poured out a glass of air and at the same time a glass of water.

By tilting A under B you can fill B with air and so you can pour the air from one glass to another. Moreover, you can pour air upwards from below.

And you have discovered how it can be made visible merely by letting it rise through water as bubbles, little silvery air balloons!

But . . . your glass is empty. Are you so thirsty? May I pour you another glass of air?

2. *Invert a glass of water without spilling a drop*

You will need: glass of water, piece of card.

Fill a drinking glass right up to the brim with water and lay on the top a piece of card or stiff paper. Hold the card on and turn the glass upside down. If you leave go of the card, the water stays in the glass and the card is not pushed off by the weight of the water. How is this possible?

The air outside exerts a pressure on the card of about $14\frac{1}{2}$ lb per square inch. The force with which the air holds the card against the glass is amply sufficient to support $1\frac{1}{2}$ times as much water as in the glass.

With a bit of skill it is possible to invert the glass of water without holding the card on with your fingers.

3. An oil tin crushed by air pressure

You will need: an oil can, water, gas flame.

'Oil can crushed by the air'—that makes us think of a sensational headline in a newspaper. It is rather sensational to be able to crush a can by air pressure in your own home.

For this impressive experiment you will need a one-gallon rectangular tin with a screw cap. One of those large cans which hold 14 lb of syrup will do excellently. If you have any suspicions at all that the can has ever held any inflammable liquid like petrol, make sure that it is thoroughly washed out beforehand so that not the slightest trace of the smell of the liquid remains. Pour into the can a good cupful of hot water, and bring it to the boil on the gas or electric stove. Let the water boil vigorously for a few minutes. The steam drives off the greater part of the air from the can. Turn off the gas and quickly screw the cap on. Now let cold water run over the can by standing it under the tap. (Take care!—The can is hot!) The steam in the can condenses to water; inside the can there is a very low pressure of air and against the outside of the can the air pressure gains the upper hand, and what happens? With loud groans and creaks the can crumples up, squeezed and crushed by the gigantic force which the air can exert.

4. How heavy air is!

You will need: wooden lath, 2 newspapers, your fist.

Did you know that a weight of 400 lb presses on your hand? And on your whole body, many thousands of pounds? You have never noticed it, eh? It really is so, you know. What is it, then,

12

that presses so heavily on us? The air again! Yes, the light-weight air. The air presses on each square inch of us with a force of $14\frac{1}{2}$ lb; that is, on an area a little bigger than a stamp. A whole hand has an area of several square inches; thus, on top of it there rests a weight of many pounds. But the air presses from all sides, and also the hand presses back, so we do not notice the air pressure.

You can show the tremendous weight of the air, in addition to doing the oil can experiment, in the following way. Lay on a strong table a thin board or lath about 4 inches by 20 inches and cover it with a newspaper. The paper must not be damaged; there must not even be a hole in it. Smooth the paper flat and then, with your fist, hit the projecting end of the lath. To your surprise you will have no success from your blow—a blow that could easily have given someone a black eye or driven them into hospital: the paper does not go up into the air. Hit as hard as you like, the paper stays quite still, but there is every chance that you will break the lath into pieces. You can strike the lath with a heavy piece of wood. The lath will snap— but the paper will stay where it is.

How does it come about that the lath stays put as though it was firmly nailed down? You will probably find that the paper is about 34 inches long and 25 inches wide, and so the area is about 850 square inches. This means that the air presses on it with a force of something like 12,325 lb!

5. Barometer and drinking fountain for birds – in one

You will need: bottle, dish of water, strip of paper.

Have you come across the kind of barometer that can also be used as a drinking fountain for birds? It is very nice for the birds because they can see at the same time what the weather is going to be . . . But seriously, you can make yourself a barometer of this sort quite easily. Fill a bottle three quarters full of water and invert it

into a basin which already has some water in it. Keep your thumb over the mouth of the bottle until it is under the water in the basin.

On the outside of the bottle stick a strip of paper with numbered marks on it. There you have the simplest form of barometer. When the air pressure is high, which usually means good weather, the water in the bottle stands high; with low pressure, usually a warning of bad weather, the water does not stand so high. The rise and fall in the water level are not very great, and changes in the temperature will make the air in the bottle expand or contract, so you must keep your barometer in some place where the temperature varies very little indeed, for instance in a cellar or under the stairs.

If you put the barometer out of doors, the birds will show an interest in it—not, I suppose, because they want to find out what the weather is going to be, but because they are thirsty. Anyone who keep birds will find this barometer is a very handy form of drinking fountain because it does not need refilling as often as the usual kind of dish.

6 Pick up teacups with a balloon
You will need: balloon, 2 teacups.

I admit that using a balloon is rather a clumsy way to pick up teacups, but it is quite amusing and therefore you should decide to try it once. In this experiment it is strictly forbidden to use the handles of the cups. Understand? Blow up the balloon slightly, and press the cups against it, as in the sketch. Then blow the balloon up further and when you have made it quite large you will find that you can let go of the cups. Now you can lift up the balloon without the cups falling off.

You want to use the newest and prettiest cups? Naturally the experiment works . . . but it works just as well with old cups as with new ones—so why take any chances?

7. A banana skins itself

You will need: bottle, banana, some methylated spirit.

Few fruits are so easily separated from their skins as a banana. A banana can even peel itself. How? By means of air pressure. Take a slightly over-ripe banana, and at one end loosen the skin a little away from the flesh. Now look for a bottle whose neck is just wide enough for the inside of the banana to get in. Put into the bottle a small amount of methylated spirit; about half a teaspoonful. Light the methylated spirit by dropping in a lighted match or a burning scrap of paper. Immediately put the end of the banana on the mouth of the bottle in such a way that the gap is completely closed by the flesh of the banana. The peel should rest against the outside of the bottle.

To your amazement you should see the bottle suck in the banana greedily with a good deal of noise. The burning meths uses up the oxygen of the air, so that the pressure inside the bottle becomes less than that outside. The result is that the air pushes the banana deeper into the bottle so that the banana is stripped of its skin. If the experiment does not work, then I recommend that you make two or three slits lengthwise in the skin beforehand.

A bottle like this, with burning meths, is also able to draw in a boiled and shelled egg. You can also use an unboiled egg if you soften the shell beforehand by soaking it in vinegar for a while.

8. A bottle? No, a fountain!

You will need: bottle, bored cork, milk straw.

Fill a bottle half full with water and put a bored cork, fitted with a milk straw, into the neck. The straw must reach well down into the bottle. Push the cork well in so that it is tight. Now blow as hard as you can through the straw and take your face away quickly, for water shoots out of the straw immediately. If the end of the straw is pressed together a little the water will spout even higher and the fountain will last longer.

The explanation of this experiment is very simple. Because of your blowing, bubbles of air rise through the water into the upper part of the bottle which already has air in it. In this space then, we now have more air and the pressure is greater than that of the air outside. When you stop blowing the compressed air pushes the water up the straw, with the result that the bottle begins to spout like a fountain.

9. Stick two glasses together with air

You will need: 2 drinking glasses, rubber ring, paper.

For this experiment you will need a rubber ring such as is used for sealing preserving jars. The ring must fit on a glass. Wet the ring and lay it on top of one of the glasses. Then drop a bit of burning tissue paper into the glass, and immediately put the other glass upside down on top. When the paper stops burning the two glasses are stuck together. If you pick up the upper glass you find that the other one is firmly stuck to it. Just as in the case of the self-skinning banana there is a reduction of air pressure inside the two glasses. It is the air outside, with its greater pressure, which presses the glasses so tightly together.

Those who like to be safe rather than sorry will use unbreakable glasses, for if you break an ordinary glass you won't be able to stick the pieces together with air!

10. Lift 20 lb of books with your breath

You will need: large paper or plastic bag, several heavy books.

Oh, get away, you'll say, you don't expect me to believe that. Tip 20 lb of books over with my breath! Quite impossible! And all your friends and family will say that it cannot be done. Unless . . . Unless you try it. Lay on the table a long, strong paper or plastic bag, about big enough to hold a large loaf. Make a good pile of books on top of it. Use the thickest and heaviest books that you can find. One pound or ten present not the slightest difficulty—your breath will lift them easily. Blow into the bag, and take care that the opening through which you blow is quite small. You can take it quite easily, no need to make a lot of effort. See—the heap of books rises.

By blowing gently you have lifted perhaps 20 lb of books with your breath—fantastic, isn't it? Take good care that the pile of books does not fall over, for they might fall on your head or face. Your breath is strong enough but could your head stand such treatment?

How is all this possible? A well-known law of nature, discovered by Pascal, states that a force on a gas (or on

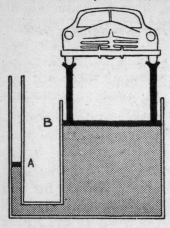

a liquid) is transmitted in all directions. Increase the force of your breath only a little, say a tenth of an atmosphere, or $1\frac{1}{2}$ lb a square inch, and then the force presses on every square inch of the paper surface of the bag, let us say 5 inches by 10 inches (50 square inches). A force of 50 × $1\frac{1}{2}$ = 75 lb. That is how the pile of books is so easily lifted.

From the same principle it is possible to explain the working of the hydraulic press or car jack which operates by liquid and not by air. Look at the second picture. If the surface of the piston B is 1,000 times greater than the surface of A, then a force of little more than 1 lb exerted on A is transmitted through the liquid so that the piston B is able to raise a load of 1,000 lb.

11. Make a pop-gun from a tube and a potato

You will need: metal or glass tube, 4″ to 6″ long, stick or pencil, slice of apple or potato.

Perhaps you think that the title must be an exaggeration. Then watch. Push the tube through a slice of raw potato. A piece of potato will stick in one end of the tube, blocking it. Do the same at the other end of the tube. With the stick, or pencil, push the first little bit of potato gently into the tube. Aim the other end of the tube at the mark you want to hit—yes, hit! For you have a potato gun in your hand. It is essentially an airgun; push hard and smartly with the stick and—POP—the other

little bit of potato shoots out like a bullet to the
target. And if you aimed well, hits it in the middle!

12. The riddle of the hovering ping-pong ball

You will need: ping-pong ball, vacuum cleaner (cylindrical type).

Have you got a vacuum cleaner of the
cylindrical type? One that you can
push the pipe into either end? I hope
so, because then you can do several interesting experiments. The first of them
is to let a ping-pong ball float in the
air. Push the pipe into the blowing end of the vacuum
cleaner and hold the free end upright. Release the ball
into the stream of air, and you will probably be surprised to see it stay there, floating freely in the air—a
really astounding performance!

Once again we have an example of the bewildering
wonders of nature. How is it that the ball remains in
the stream of air?

The air which is blown out by the vacuum cleaner is
moving very rapidly. There is a well-known law of
nature, Bernoulli's Law (discovered by a Swiss,
Bernoulli) which states: as the speed of a liquid or gas
increases so the pressure of the liquid or gas decreases.
In the rapidly moving air which is coming out of the
vacuum cleaner, the pressure is less than in the still air
which surrounds it. The ball is pushed upwards by the
stream of air; it stays up because the weight of the ball
and the force of the air against it are equal. The ball
cannot get out of the way because, outside the airstream, the pressure is greater. The result is that the
ball floats in the airstream at a fairly steady height.

Instead of the ping-pong ball you can float a blown-
up balloon, which is also heavier than air. On to the
mouth of the balloon fasten several paper clips to
prevent its being blown too far. Hold the end of the
pipe slanting upwards and the balloon, or the ball,

stays suspended in the slanting airstream—a really astonishing sight.

13. What do the apples do?

You will need: 2 apples, 2 pieces of string.

Hang two apples on strings about a yard long and about a couple of inches apart. What do you think will happen if you now blow very hard between the apples? Will they move further apart? Will the apples be pushed apart because of the stream of air? Of course, says common sense.

But common sense is wrong. You blow, and . . . as by an invisible hand the apples are drawn together! What is the explanation?

The Law of Bernoulli! As the speed of the air increases, so the pressure of the air decreases. When you blow, the air between the apples moves, so that the air pressure there is less than on the other sides of the apples where the air is still. So the air on the sides of the apples pushes them towards the region of lower pressure: the apples go together.

14. How does an aeroplane fly?

You will need: book, sheet of paper.

When Bernoulli found out, about 200 years ago, that the pressure of the air decreased according to the speed, he never realised that the law he had discovered would be the key to air travel.

If you hold in front of your mouth a thin sheet of paper it

hangs quite limp. What will happen if you blow along the upper side of the paper? The unexpected behaviour of the apples may help you to think twice before answering without thinking carefully. So—try it again. Once more the unexpected happens: the piece of paper rises into a horizontal position.

We can explain this easily. Because of your blowing there is an area of low pressure above the paper. Under the paper the air is not moving and so the pressure remains normal. Thus, the pressure under the paper is greater than it is above and, as a result, the paper is pushed upwards into a horizontal position.

You can also demonstrate this phenomenon with a book, a sheet of paper and a fan or a vacuum cleaner arranged to blow. Take a somewhat heavier sheet of paper and bend it a bit first so that the lifting power is at its greatest.

From this experiment it is a short step to the wing of a flying aeroplane. Do you follow me? Look, here you see the section of an aeroplane's wing. The upper side is curved, or arched, and the underside is straight or nearly so. The propeller, or airscrew, pulls the aircraft at high speed through the air. Air rushes past the wing at great speed. Now the air which passes over the curved upperside of the wing must travel a much greater distance in the same time than the air which passes below the wing. That means that the air going over the top of the wing travels faster than the air beneath. According to Bernoulli's Law, greater speed means a lower pressure. The air pressure under the wing is greater than the air pressure above it. The result is that the wing, and consequently the whole aeroplane, is pushed upwards and so the heavier-than-air machine is held up in the air.

15. A snake-windmill for the top of the radiator

You will need: pencil, empty cotton reel, thimble, piece of very stiff paper, piece of tinfoil, pair of scissors, pin.

When a glider, which has no engine, is in the air can it climb higher? The answer is yes, for often there are rising currents of warm air (called thermals) which make gliders rise.

Warm air is less dense than cold air and it rises just like a cork which, when released under water, rises to the top because cork is less dense than water. Warm, rising air currents originate over cornfields and tarred roads because the sun makes them hotter than the surrounding grassland. Similarly we get thermals above beaches and sand dunes because the sand becomes hotter than the seawater.

In our rooms too, we have warm, rising air over stoves and radiators. Hold over a stove a small piece of thin, light paper and let go. Notice that it is driven upwards. Just as the wind makes the sails of a windmill turn round, so can the warm, rising air above a stove start a light windmill turning. Would you like to make such a windmill?

Let us begin with a really strange model windmill—a snake! On a piece of stiff paper draw a spiral ending with a snake's head—look at the picture. Cut it out along the line. You must make it big enough for a thimble to pass through the hole shown in black.

The most convenient way to make a stand for it is as follows: take a cotton reel and stick into it one of those pencils which have a small india rubber at the top. Into the rubber stick a pin and on the top put the thimble with the paper snake. Put the whole thing on the edge of the mantelpiece, or anywhere above the stove or radiator. You will see the snake start to turn round and round. The warm, rising air pushes against the spiral and causes it to rotate. You can also make it turn by holding a lighted candle under it.

You can make a real windmill from a piece of stiff metal foil. Cut vanes in it as in the picture, twist the vanes slightly at an angle and make a small dent in the centre with the head of a pin. Mount the windmill on the top of the 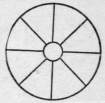 pin on the stand, and it will spin round merrily over the radiator.

The warm, rising air goes along the ceiling to the windows where it is so strongly cooled that it sinks down again to the floor. It goes along the floor to the stove or radiator and rises up again because of the heat. This is the cause of the circulation of the air which ventilates the room.

16. Make yourself a hot-air balloon

You will need: a light paper bag or 6 sheets of thin tissue paper, gum or paste, wire, cotton wool, methylated spirit or a Meta solid fuel block.

On the 21st November 1793 two young French noble-men, Pilâtre de Rozier and the Duc d'Arlandes, stepped into a basket in which there was a stove with an open top. The basket hung from a linen-lined paper bag, 58 feet across, manufactured by the Montgolfier papermakers. The paper bag became filled with hot air which was warmer than the surrounding air and the result was that the bag with its basket and two passengers rose upwards. This was the first time in history that men lifted themselves into the atmosphere.

The modern air balloon is filled with gas; but you can get a lot of amusement out of making an old-fashioned hot-air balloon from a paper bag.

To do this take a large, light paper bag. From thin

wire you can make a simple basket (see the drawing), of which the upper ring is the same size as the mouth of  the bag. With a few small bits of wire, or strips of sticky tape, you can hang the little basket under the bag. In the basket lay a tin lid with a wad of cotton wool damped with meths, or a block of solid fuel such as Meta, which is set alight. Seeing that there is always the chance that the paper bag may catch fire this experiment must always be done in the open air. Even so, with quite a small block of Meta, in still air the balloon can rise very high.

A hot air balloon with a better shape, which will give decidedly better results, can be made from six sheets of tissue paper. This is cut to the shape shown in the sketch. The six sheets are gummed together so as  to make a balloon. A circular piece is gummed to the top.

The lifting power of such a balloon can be very great. A kite string can be tied to the balloon to prevent its drifting away and getting lost. Anyone who is really handy can make a balloon a yard in diameter from somewhat stronger paper. This would of course need a much larger fire.

17. Make yourself a boomerang

You will need: piece of 3-ply wood or thick cardboard.

In spite of their ignorance of science the aborigines of Australia managed to produce a first-class weapon— the boomerang. Here you can see the shape of it—it could not be simpler. If such a boomerang is held by one end between finger and thumb, so that the other end is towards you, and is thrown away at a slight slope, then it describes a curved path through the air and soon returns to you.

You can make a boomerang like this from a piece of plywood. Each arm is about 10 inches long. Round off all the edges with glass paper. When you have got the shape right, throw it in the correct manner and it should come back to you. The Australians hunt birds with it; and obviously it must be very convenient, for if it misses its target it comes back to the hunter. You can also make a boomerang in lighter material, e.g. from cardboard, or a bigger one using heavier material. Try experimenting with them.

18. What does the sheet of paper do?

You will need: 2 books, sheet of paper.

Over two books lying a short distance apart, lay a sheet of paper. What happens if you blow underneath the paper? Does the paper fly away?

Hard luck! The paper drops down. Can you understand how that happens? If not, think about Mr. Bernoulli.

19. What do the sheets of paper do?

You will need: 2 sheets of writing paper.

When you hold two pieces of paper firmly and blow between them, what happens? Do you blow the papers apart? Try it and once again you will see something you probably did not expect: the two sheets go towards each other.

Explanation: The same happens here as with the apples. Following the law of Bernoulli, between the papers there is a reduction in air pressure; the force of the air on the outer sides of the papers is greater than the force of the air between them, so that the papers are pushed inwards.

20. Make yourself an atomiser

You will need: 2 glass tubes or drinking straws, glass of water.

Stand one of the glass tubes or a transparent straw upright in a half-filled glass of water. You will notice that the water stands as high in the tube as it does in the glass.

Now hold close to the top of the tube and at right-angles to its upper end, a second tube, and blow through it. The water level rises in the upright tube, a clear proof that the fast flowing stream of air produces a reduction in air pressure. Blow very hard and the water rises to the opening and so we can 'atomise' the water into fine droplets.

Paint sprays, insect sprays and scent sprays work in precisely the same manner. They are all based on the phenomenon discovered by Bernoulli, but in these the human mouth, which blows, is replaced by a rubber ball which is squeezed. Instead of the ball a tube with a sucker can be used as a pump, or a reservoir of compressed air will give a continuous supply.

21. How much oxygen does the air contain?

You will need: milk bottle, saucer or bowl of water, candle, matches.

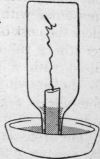

Stand the candle on the bottom of the bowl, making sure that a good part of it is well clear of the water. Light the candle and quickly (but not so quickly that the flame is put out by the draught) place a milk bottle over the candle. The candle continues to burn, but the flame gradually gets smaller and smaller until it eventually goes out. As the

26

flame dies down you will see the water rising in the bottle till it reaches a height of about one-quarter of the bottle.

Why does the candle go out? Through lack of oxygen. Burning is simply a chemical combination between the material and the oxygen of the air, setting free heat in the process. The free oxygen is used up and is bound chemically to the burnable material. From the air in the bottle most of the oxygen is used up, and when this happens the candle cannot burn any longer. At the same time the pressure of the air in the bottle is reduced because part of it has been used. Water occupies the place of the vanished oxygen and fills about one-fifth of the volume of the bottle. But we must remember that the flame heated the air, making it expand, and when the air cooled again it contracted, causing more water to enter the bottle than the volume of the used-up oxygen.

22. Measure the proportion of oxygen with rusting iron

You will need: small medicine bottle, glass tube, bored cork, glass of water, some steel wool or iron filings, some vinegar.

What is rusting? A sort of slow burning of iron without a flame, for when iron rusts it combines chemically with oxygen. Now, rusting iron gives us a much better opportunity to show that about one-fifth of the air consists of oxygen.

In the bottom of the small medicine bottle put some steel wool or iron filings previously moistened with some water and vinegar. Then close the neck of the bottle with a cork, or better still a rubber stopper, bored and fitted with a glass tube as you see in the drawing. Put the open end of the tube in a glass which is half full of water.

The iron starts to rust and uses up the oxygen of the air in the bottle. This happens quite slowly. And all the while the water gradually rises up the tube. In the end all the oxygen is used up and then about one-fifth of the volume of the tube and bottle is filled with water.

23. Make yourself a weather house

You will need: Some thin plywood or cardboard, some human hair or a gut violin string, screw eye, cork, some gum or glue.

Nowadays the weather forecast comes to us in the papers, over the radio and by television—the old-fashioned weather house has been pensioned off. For all that it is still quite pleasant to make one, for the weather report and the weather situation may differ quite a lot. By watching how far the little man with his umbrella or the little woman with her sunshade comes out, we can judge what the weather is likely to be.

The weather house reacts only to the dampness of the air, while a barometer records the air pressure. You can make your weather house from either ply-wood or cardboard. The external decorations I leave entirely to you. The part that reacts to the amount of mois-ture in the air is simply a single human hair, or a piece of violin string made of pre-pared gut. One end of the hair or gut is stuck to a little  cork in which a small hole has been bored. The other end is tied to a little screw eye which is fixed into a small piece of wood. On the piece of wood are glued the two little figures, which are made from plywood or cardboard. You must make quite sure that the figures balance each other perfectly so that the board hangs horizontally. By screwing the eye slightly into or out of the board you can 'set' the house so that in dry, sunny weather the little woman comes out, and in damp weather the man comes out.

24. Do you know the weather picture?

You will need: coloured picture, blotting paper, water, some cobalt chloride and cooking salt.

Do you remember the weather pictures, the brightly coloured pictures on which the blue turns pink in damp weather? Pictures like these can be made quite easily. Dissolve in some water two teaspoonfuls of cobalt chloride and one of cooking salt. In the solution soak a piece of new, white blotting paper. While the paper is damp it is pink. Let it dry in the sunshine or near the fire and it changes to blue. Now you must make a coloured picture, for example a seaside, or a mountain scene. Over the blue of the sky stick your piece of blotting paper. In dry weather the sky is bright blue, but when damp weather is coming we are warned in good time because the sky turns pink.

25. The leaves of plants produce oxygen in sunlight

You will need: preserving jar or large jam jar, funnel, test tube, some water weed, and a long wooden splint.

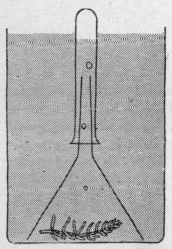

Through the effect of sunlight green plants change carbon dioxide into oxygen. You can demonstrate this with some water weed laid on the bottom of a large jam jar full of water with a funnel inverted over it. Then over the funnel invert a test tube completely full of water. Stand the jar in strong sunlight and you will see how tiny bubbles of gas rise up out of the plant and displace the water in the

29

test tube. When nearly all the water has been driven out of the test tube (and this may take some hours), take your splint, light it, and a few seconds later blow it out. Take the test tube out of the water, keeping your thumb over the open end and turn it the right way up. Remove your thumb and insert the glowing splint. The splint bursts into flame: a proof that the gas in the test tube is oxygen.

26. A flour bomb as a noisy finale to our air experiments

You will need: large tin (eg. a 2 lb syrup tin), candle, some dry flour, funnel, rubber tube and some matches.

Can flour burn? If you tried to set fire to a small heap of flour you would not succeed. But finely divided flour in a cloud—that can make a completely harmless bomb! In the bottom of a large tin bore a hole that the rubber tube will just fit into. In this end of the tube put a funnel and into it put a teaspoonful of flour. On

 the bottom of the tin put a burning candle. Put the lid on the tin and immediately blow strongly into the rubber tube. With a great BANG! off flies the lid of the tin. The finely divided flour has exploded.

It is best to do this experiment out of doors. Not that the explosion is dangerous, but the lid might go through a window or do some damage in the room. It is also important to take care that the lid does not hit you in the face. Given reasonable care this flour bomb explosion is perfectly harmless.

Attractive experiments

More than two thousand years ago the shepherd boy Magnes was tending his flock. With him he had a long stick with an iron point. As he stood watching his sheep he rested his stick on a piece of rock. When he wanted to fetch back a sheep which had wandered too far away he found, to his great surprise, that the iron tip of his staff was held fast to the rock. From this rock there came a mysterious force which attracted iron objects.

Magnes was the first to find this kind of rock. Later on others also found pieces of rock which attracted iron objects. Because Magnes was their discoverer, such pieces of stone have been called magnets.

Or do magnets derive their name from the district in Greece in which the pieces of magnetic rock were first found and which was called Magnesia? We don't know....

Once upon a time . . . there was in China a monarch called Hoangti who found himself with his army on the vast plains in a thick mist. This happened while he was pursuing his mortal enemy, a prince who had tried to drive him from the throne. Which way must he go? The king was able to find the way. He had with him a carriage in which was a statue of a woman with an outstretched arm which could rotate freely. The arm always pointed to the North, and although the men could hardly see a thing through the mist, thanks to that statue they could find the direction in which the enemy must have fled. This is a legend, but it is founded on fact. In that statue there must have been a magnet; and we know that thousands of years ago Chinese travellers made use of pivoted, magnetised needles in order to find their way through the vast Chinese empire.

About 600 years ago, men in Europe made use of the magnetic needle in the form of the compass for their sea voyages. This had far-reaching results. Previously the sailors had not ventured far from the coasts for fear of losing their way on the boundless ocean. With the magnetic pathfinder they now dared to cross over the oceans. This led to Columbus's discovery of America and to voyages by the Dutch, Portuguese and English to South Africa, India, Indonesia and Australia.

THIS SIMPLE MAGNETIC NEEDLE PROVED TO BE A KEY WHICH UNLOCKED THE WHOLE WORLD!

A magnet is a thing which is able to draw iron articles towards it. The attractive force, which comes from the magnet, is known as magnetism.

Some pieces of iron ore form *natural magnets*.

The best known artificially made magnets are the *horse shoe magnet* in the shape of a U and the *bar magnet*.

If you hold such a magnet above some iron nails, paper clips or needles they are drawn towards the ends of the magnet.

The ends of a magnet are called the *poles*. The attractive force is strongest at the poles.

The middle of the magnet is not magnetic at all.

Hang from a magnetic pole a nail (which has not

been itself magnetised) and hold beneath the nail a smaller nail or a needle; it is attracted by the larger nail. Under the influence of the magnet the larger nail has become magnetised. If you take the nail away from the magnet it is no longer a magnet. The iron remains unmagnetised.

A steel bar or a needle can be magnetised by stroking it several times in the same direction with one pole of a magnet. Steel does not lose its magnetism as iron does, but remains magnetised.

If you hang a magnetised needle so that it can turn round freely then it always sets in a North-South direction. Such a needle is called a compass needle. The pole which points to the North is called the North pole, the other the South pole. The instrument in which this needle is fixed is called a *compass*.

THE COMPASS IS THE FAITHFUL AND INDISPENSABLE GUIDE AND COMPANION OF EVERY SAILOR AND AIRMAN

27. Make yourself a compass

You will need: needle, magnet, cork, saucer of water, some paper and a pencil, scissors and a ruler.

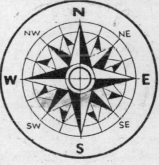

Although we do not intend to cross the ocean next week-end it is still worth while making a compass. For this you must first of all make a magnetic needle. I will repeat the instructions again: several times in succession stroke the needle in the same direction with one pole of the magnet. After each stroke lift the magnet and bring it back to the starting point in an arc.

The very simplest way to make this magnetised needle act as a compass needle is to lay it very carefully on a saucer of water. But, surely, a needle like

33

that never floats, for isn't steel much heavier than water? Steel is indeed much heavier than water; nevertheless a steel needle can float on water, and it does so because of the so-called 'surface tension' of water. That is to say, water acts as if it possesses a 'skin' which is not broken if the needle is laid on the surface very gently. Now it is able to turn round into a North-South direction.

The compass we are going to make will be a bit more elaborate, however. First, cut a slice about half an inch thick from a wide cork. Push the needle through it along a diameter. From white paper or card cut a round disc and exactly in the centre of it draw two lines at right angles. On the end of one of the lines draw an arrow and write N beside it. At the ends of the other lines put S, W and E. Now put the slice of cork with the needle in it into a china or glass saucer containing water. The cork turns round until the needle points North and South. But how can you find out which is the end that points to the North? In your

own house you should know where North is. If not you can easily find where South is; it is where the sun is at mid-day. As soon as you know which end points North stick the disc with glue, or fasten it with two small brass drawing pins, to the top surface of the cork. The North-South line must be in line with the needle, the N over the north end of the needle.

If you want to make your compass more like the big compasses, you can draw a compass rose on the disc—see the sketch.

28. Magnet poles can be 'attractive' and 'repulsive'

You will need: 2 bar or horseshoe magnets.

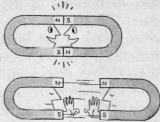

Yes, magnets are more human than you had thought; their poles can attract each other as well as repel each other. If you hold two magnets with their poles together it is possible they will attract each other with quite a strong force and jump together with a click, but it is also possible that a mysterious, unseen hand will push them apart.

By hanging a magnet up so that it can turn round freely you can find out which is the North pole and which is the South. You can mark the North pole by scratching an N or sticking a bit of gummed paper on it. If you now bring one end of a magnet up to one pole of another magnet you will find that the North and South poles attract each other and that a North pole repels another North pole. Similarly two South poles repel each other.

Like poles repel; unlike poles attract.

Another way to show this is as follows: down through the centres of two thin slices of cork push magnetised needles, having marked which ends are North poles and which are South. You can find out which poles are which by holding the needles close to your compass. Remember that like poles repel. Let the needles float in water so that the North poles are above the surface and the South poles are below. Then you will see the corks move apart, each repelled by the other. But turn one cork upside down, then the corks go together—attracting each other!

29. Make little magnetic boats

You will need: strong magnet, aluminium cake tin or dish of water, wood, nails.

Magnetic boats . . . that sounds mysterious. And indeed it can appear very mysterious. At the beginning of this century there was exhibited at Amsterdam a little boat which circled endlessly on a pond, although it had no motor or other form of propulsion in it and was not pulled by a thread. Thousands of visitors asked themselves how the little boat could keep on going. But it was very simple. The boat was made of iron, and under the pond in which it sailed was a powerful magnet on a large horizontal disc. The disc rotated slowly, driven by an electric motor, and the boat followed the path of the magnet.

You can make something like this on a smaller scale. From soft wood cut out several little boats not more than $1\frac{1}{2}$ inches long. In the back of each boat push a 1 inch nail. Bore a hole in the deck to take a match and stick a triangle of paper on it, then you have a sailing boat. Put the boats in the water and slowly draw the magnet along underneath the dish. In this way you can make the boats sail round quite nicely. You could also make a wooden disc on which you can lay the magnet. Through the middle of the disc goes an axle on which you can fix a small pulley wheel. Then you can make the disc rotate slowly by means of a small electric motor.

30. Fishing with a magnetic fishing rod

You will need: stick, piece of string, aluminium pan or bowl, or aquarium tank or washbowl, some cardboard or thin wood, some paper clips, pair of scissors, small horseshoe magnet.

Fishing with a magnetic fishing rod is quite possible provided that you look for iron fish! Cut some fish out of cardboard or thin wood. With cardboard fish one or more paperclips will have to be used to make the weight right. The fish must neither float nor sink, but must stay suspended in the water. You can fix a bit of tinplate round the wooden fishes.

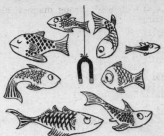

Your fishing rod is made from a stick to which a piece of string is tied. A horseshoe magnet is tied to the other end of the string. Then the children can go fishing.

31. How to show a magnet's 'fingerprints'

You will need: horseshoe magnet, sheet of paper, some iron filings, a few books.

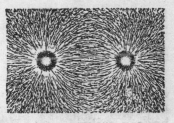

With the help of two small piles of books you can fix the magnet upright with the poles at the top. Over them lay a sheet of paper, and sprinkle some iron filings lightly on top. The little particles of iron set themselves in curved lines spreading out from the poles of the magnet. These lines are known as *lines of force;* they show the directon of the magnetic attraction. By tapping on the paper very gently you can improve the appearance of the lines.

The curved lines formed by the iron filings certainly have the appearance of fingerprints, and so it is not too fanciful to speak of a magnet's 'fingerprints'. If you have two magnets you can make quite a different set of fingerprints appear. Lay the two magnets down flat, close enough for you to feel the force of repulsion between them. They must therefore have like poles facing each other. Over the magnets lay a sheet of paper and sprinkle iron filings on it. The filings set themselves in patterns which clearly demonstrate that like poles repel each other. Quite a different pattern appears if you reverse the position of one magnet so that unlike poles are opposite each other. It is wise to put a piece of wood or card between the magnets now, or they may jump together.

Instead of paper you could use a sheet of glass for this experiment.

32. Heat destroys magnetism

You will need: 2 magnetised needles, 1 compass.

 If you hold a magnetised needle beside a compass needle then one end of the compass needle turns away from the little magnet. But if beforehand, you hold the needle in a gas flame until it becomes red hot and then let it cool down, you will find that the magnetism has gone. (What happens is that both ends of the compass are attracted.) Also, if you hit the needle several times with a hammer you will find that the magnetism has gone, or is very much weakened.

If you break a magnetised needle in half you will find that each piece is a complete magnet in itself, with a North and a South pole. You can prove this by holding a piece near to a compass. If you break one of these halves in two again, once more you have two complete little magnets. And so you could go on.

What is the explanation? You can imagine that iron, like steel, consists of extremely small bar magnets. Each of these magnets is so small that it cannot be seen. In the drawings, however, these magnets are shown diagrammatically. In magnetised steel all the magnets lie in the same direction, and always with a North pole to the South pole of the next magnet. In the middle of the magnet all the South poles cancel out all the North poles and so the magnet is not magnetic in the middle. But at the ends there are either all South poles or all North poles, so that at these places the magnetism is strongest.

From the drawing you can see immediately how the breaking of a magnet into two pieces results in two complete magnets, and that no matter how often a magnet is broken each small piece is a complete magnet.

In unmagnetised steel and iron the little magnets lie quite haphazardly, so that all together they give out no 'magnetic force'. When the iron or steel is magnetised, all the little magnets are drawn into lines in the same direction. They all have their North poles at the same ends. In steel the little magnets remain in these positions; in iron, on the other hand, they rapidly become disorganised again, so that the iron does not remain magnetised once the force of another magnet is removed. Steel remains magnetised until, as you have seen, it is hammered. Because of the blows the tiny magnets soon become upset and take up their irregular positions once more. The same thing happens when the steel is heated.

Experiments with forces

ISAAC NEWTON (1642-1725), *the great English mathematician, scientist and astronomer:*

'The third law of motion, which I have discovered, states: *Every action has an equal and opposite reaction.* If you push with your finger against a stone, gentlemen, then the stone pushes back with an equal force against your finger.'

Demonstration 1. Have you ever wanted to jump from the side of a rowing boat on to the land? Before you can do it you must, according to Newton's Law, push the boat backwards. And what happens then? In you go!

Demonstration 2.

33. Railway lines push the train forwards

You will need: toy engine, 2 rails, strip of three-ply, 6 round pencils.

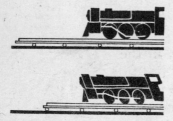

In order for a train to move, the rails must push forward as hard as the train pushes backward. You don't believe it?—You can demonstrate it for yourself. It is probable that you have not got a real locomotive at your disposal, so you will have to carry out your demonstration with a toy one. Lay a couple of rails on a strip of three-ply, hardboard or stout cardboard, and put the engine on the rails. Under the board put six round pencils or pieces of dowelling.

When you switch on, or release the brake, the engine goes forward, but . . . the rails go backward!

Demonstration 3.

The recoil of a gun

Demonstration 4.

34. Make a cannon from a bottle

You will need: empty bottle, some vinegar, some baking powder, a paper serviette, 2 round pencils.

Put into the bottle just enough vinegar so that none runs out when the bottle is laid on its side. Roll a teaspoonful of baking powder in a paper serviette, twist the ends tightly and push the paper 'bomb' into the bottle. Quickly put the cork in and lay the bottle on the two round pencils. Because of the pressure produced by the carbon dioxide which is generated, the cork is blown out of the bottle with a bang while the bottle runs backwards just like a real cannon.

35. How a jet plane flies

You will need: ordinary balloon.

Blow up the balloon and hold the end tightly with your fingers. Now, in the balloon there is a higher air pressure than in the air around it which pushes the rubber outwards with equal pressure in all directions. So the balloon gets its shape—a large ball.

What happens if you now suddenly let go of the balloon? Try it! The balloon shoots away in the opposite direction to the air escaping from the mouth. This agrees completely with Newton's Third Law. The air escaping backwards produces a force also acting backwards. A forward reaction follows, and so the balloon moves in a forward direction. You can also think of it like this: the air escaping backwards pushes against the balloon and so the balloon goes forwards. While the balloon was held tightly, the air was pressing strongly and equally against the inside. The forces inside were in equilibrium, cancelling each other out, and so the balloon had no tendency to move. But the moment you opened the outlet the equilibrium was disturbed. The air pressure against the front of the balloon was no longer in equilibrium with the pressure against the back of the balloon and so it forced the balloon forwards. The different explanations which have been given for the forward movement of the balloon really amount to the same thing.

Now, perhaps, you will ask: what has all this got to do with a jet plane? A jet plane isn't a balloon, is it? In a jet plane there is a combustion chamber which is open at the back. By burning a certain kind of fuel, hot gases at high pressure are produced in it. The gases can only escape in a backward direction. The backward forces, which are set up, have a forward reaction as a result of which the aircraft is pushed forwards. Rockets work in the same way. It is not that the escaping gases press against the surrounding air, as many people suppose. The rocket works best in airless space because there is no air resistance to act as a brake.

36. Make a jet boat from an egg

You will need: some stiff paper, some glue (or balsa cement), an egg shell, 2 pipe cleaners, a large cork, some cotton wool and methylated spirit, small tin lid, a dish of water.

We are going to make a steam boat which, since it follows the principle by which the jet plane works, can be called a 'jet boat'.

Begin by making a boat from some stiff paper; see the drawing. A small piece of paper will serve as a rudder. Make a small hole in it  and two small holes in the stern. Then by means of a thread you can set the rudder in position so that it goes round in a circle.

Over the sides lay two pipe cleaners which have been bent so that an egg can lie snugly in them. Now you must empty an egg without breaking the shell. To do this prick a small hole in each end of the egg. Blow through one hole and the contents of the egg will come out through the other hole. Once the egg is empty you can seal one hole with glue, balsa cement or sealing wax. Half fill the shell with water and lay it on the wires with the hole at the stern. Your boiler is now complete.

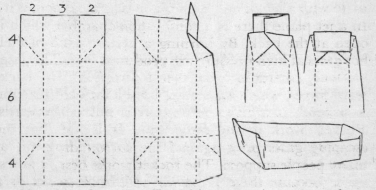

Now the furnace! For this you can use an almost burnt out nightlight or a small tin lid with a piece of candle or a bit of cotton wool soaked in methylated spirit. Put the little boat on the water and light the fire. After a little while the water boils and a jet of steam spurts out of the hole in the eggshell. This backward-moving jet of steam causes a reaction which forces the little boat forward. Then it will go round gaily.

37. Make a jet boat from a powder tin

You will need: metal soap dish, empty powder tin, some wire or 4 pipe cleaners, stump of candle or a nightlight.

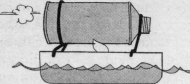

There is still another way to make a jet boat—from an empty powder or metal polish tin.

Bore a small hole in the bottom of the powder tin near to the side, and fill the tin about half full with hot water. Mount the tin with the aid of some wire or pipecleaners, with the little hole at the top, on top of one half of the soap dish. Light the candle or nightlight and put it under the boiler. As soon as the water boils, a jet of steam escapes from the hole and the little ship is driven forwards.

Handy 'Hobbyists' can think of a number of variations in the construction of jet boats. For instance, a wooden boat can be made with an empty tin mounted on top.

38. Make a glass steam turbine

You will need: glass tube, piece of wire, nightlight or spirit lamp.

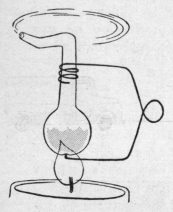

Take a thin glass tube and heat it in a gas flame until one end is sealed. Then heat the end again and blow a small bulb on it with a diameter of about $\frac{3}{4}''$. While you are doing this keep the tube rotating in the flame. When you blow the bulb take it out of the flame. Let it cool slowly, holding the tube near the flame. While the bulb is cooling, but before it hardens, press with a pencil point against the underside of the bulb to make a little dent in it. Heat the tube again, above the bulb, and bend it at right angles in the middle. Close to the open end do the same thing again so that finally the tube has the shape shown in the picture. The nozzle can be made by softening the end in the flame and pulling it out with a clothes peg. Lastly make from iron or copper wire a holder in which the whole thing can rotate.

Fill the little bulb by warming it and holding the nozzle under water. Do not fill it more than half way. Hold a small flame under it, and when the water boils steam will come out of the nozzle and the 'steam turbine' will spin round. Here again it is the reaction-force which sets the thing in motion. Revolving lawn sprinklers work on the same principle.

39. More force is needed to start a thing than to keep it moving

You will need: toy motor car, elastic band.

That a greater force is needed to start a car moving than to keep it moving can be demonstrated with a fairly heavy toy car or truck, by pulling it with an elastic band. When getting it into motion, i.e. starting it, the elastic band is stretched more than when the

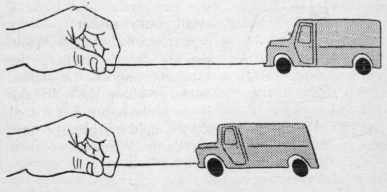

car is moving. In a real car there is a gearbox which is really a sort of 'retarder'. It converts the high revolutions of the engine into lower revolutions which, however, produce a greater force—the force which is necessary to put the car into motion.

What applies to a toy car also applies to all cars and other bodies: in order to get them moving, a certain 'unwillingness to move' has to be overcome. Newton called this 'unwillingness-to-move' Inertia. Inertia can be observed in very many ways, e.g. if you want to start a heavy barrow moving, or if you try to start pedalling a heavily laden bicycle, it takes much force and effort, but once it is moving, it is not so difficult to keep it moving. But if we want to stop something we again notice this unwillingness, this inertia. While we are stopping, the car, the barrow, or the heavily laden bicycle seems to have a desire to keep going. Bringing a body from a state of rest into motion, or from motion to a state of rest, needs much more force than keeping in motion a body already moving.

40. Inertia is a wonderful thing

You will need: glass of water, sheet of paper.

'Yes. This inertia is a wonderful thing!' said the boy sitting lazily in the easy chair. 'I have absolutely no need to demonstrate what Newton called the "Law of Inertia". I feel it so well. . . .'

So now let's jerk this lazy fellow into action by showing him a wonderful experiment. On a sheet of paper stand a glass of water which is perfectly dry on the outside. If the glass is not dry then the trick won't work. Ask your friends if they think it is possible to get the glass off the paper without touching the glass. If they say 'Yes', then how? Perhaps one will try to pull the paper, very slowly and carefully, away from under the glass, but he is sure to fail. What, however, can be done is to pull the paper away from under the

glass with a sharp jerk. The glass stays where it is because of its inertia. But you must not hesitate! Only by pulling the paper away very smartly will you be successful. It is advisable to use an unbreakable glass, at any rate while you are practising, in case you hesitate.

41. Which string will you break? You can choose

You will need: heavy book, piece of thin string.

Cut the string in two and hang up a heavy book with one half. Tie the other piece to the underside of the book. By pulling steadily downwards on the lower string you can make the upper string break. But if you want to break the lower string then you must give a sharp tug. The inertia of the book prevents the full force of the tug from reaching the upper string.

42. Which egg is the boiled one?

You will need: raw egg, hard (not soft) boiled egg, 2 saucers.

By making an egg spin round you can find out if it is raw or boiled. It may happen some day in the kitchen that nobody can remember which of two eggs has been boiled, and then this method is very handy for finding out. Spin each egg on a plate or saucer by giving it a smart twist. The egg which spins the longer is the boiled one. The raw egg spins most reluctantly; it wobbles and soon falls over.

Now spin the eggs again, but suddenly seize each egg and stop it spinning. Immediately, however, let them both go again. The hardboiled egg then remains motionless on the plate, but the raw egg actually begins to spin round again by itself. . . .

The explanation of the strange behaviour of the raw egg? The contents of the raw egg are liquid. Because of inertia the innermost layers of the liquid contents cannot follow the rapid motion and so they slide over the outermost layers. Inside the egg so much friction is set up that it stays spinning for only a short time. But that does not mean that the inside layers have stopped already. It is because of this that the egg starts to spin again all by itself when you let go of it.

43. Obedient and disobedient eggs

You will need: 2 blown egg shells, some sand, iron filings and glue, a piece of paper.

Let an egg which you have blown, dry out, and then close one opening with glue or sealing wax.

When you have boiled eggs for breakfast you can produce one that you have prepared beforehand with some sand inside. Then you can bewilder your table companions with your egg which is so obedient that it will remain in any position in which you put it. It stays standing quietly on top of the salt cellar. It can stand on its point without any assistance from the resourceful Columbus. (Do you know the story of Columbus and the egg?) You can make it balance on all sorts of sloping surfaces provided that they are not too slippery. The egg can just as easily stand upright as slanting. But in order to make it do what you want it to, you must always put it in the position you want it to maintain and then tap it very gently. The sand settles horizontally, the egg is heavier below and lighter on top and so it stays in any chosen position.

Obedience is an old-fashioned idea that many a youngster might well acquire.

But now, without undermining discipline . . . the disobedient egg! For this you must make a rather bigger hole in the shell. Through it pour some iron filings until the shell is about one-sixth full. Then squeeze some glue from a tube through the hole so that it falls upon the iron filings. Let the glue dry, then seal up the hole.

In what way is this egg disobedient? Lay it down in a horizontal position, and immediately it rights itself. Set it on its point with the heavy end upwards. It will roll over and stand with the point upwards. In whatever position you put it, it will always return to the same position. The egg is extraordinarily disobedient. But do not punish it, for it cannot help itself.

By painting a face on the egg, you can make a very amusing tumbler for the children.

44. Which way will the lath fall?

You will need: a lath 2 to 3 feet long.

At first this experiment does not seem to be very interesting, but in fact it is one of the most surprising experiments in this book. Over the outstretched forefingers of both your hands lay a lath so that one end stands out further than the other. Now, this is the question: if you bring your two hands together, slowly, which way will the lath fall? Naturally you expect that the lath will fall on that side where the projecting end is longer. That seems as clear as daylight. But, as you bring your two hands slowly together, something happens that is quite different from what you expect. The stick does not fall at all, but remains in equilibrium. And as your fingers meet, notice that the lath rests exactly at its centre, balanced on your fingers. And no matter how often you do it, or with whatever kind of stick or lath, the same thing always happens! The stick always slides so that it automatically stays in equilibrium!

It is friction which accounts for this behaviour. The end which sticks out further presses with a greater force on the finger than the shorter end does. The greater force causes greater friction, so that there is no sliding at this spot for the moment. The lath only slides at the place with less pressure and less friction, and that is the finger near the shorter end. When the pressure on both fingers is equal—and that is the case when both sides are the same length—the lath also slides on the first finger. And so one side is as long as the other, and the lath remains in equilibrium.

45. Two forks as balancing artists on a needle point

You will need: large cork, 2 forks, needle, pencil.

If you look at the drawing you may hardly believe that such a balancing feat is possible. And yet it is really quite simple to do. Into a cork stick two forks and a needle. Hold a pencil in your hand with the point upwards and put the point of the needle on it. The whole thing remains nicely in equilibrium. You can even make the cork and the needle spin round on the point of the pencil. Eventually you may be able, just like the clown, to let the pencil balance on your nose. But remember that forks can have sharp prongs. I prefer to hold the pencil in my hand.

46. Balance a cup on your finger with the aid of two knives

You will need: 2 knives, cup, roll of paper.

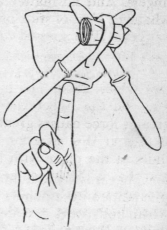

With the help of a little roll of paper fix two knives in the handle of a cup as you see in the picture. Stand the cup on the tip of your outstretched finger: it is almost as safe there as it would be in the middle of the table. If the handles of the knives are heavy enough, it should be possible to fill the cup with tea without upsetting it.

47. The tightrope-dancing bottle

You will need: string, bottle, umbrella, some chalk.

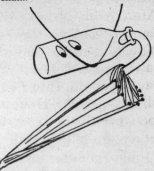

Make a loosely stretched string stiffish by rubbing it with chalk. There is nothing dishonest in doing this, for real tightrope walkers do it too, only they rub the chalk on the soles of their shoes. Push the handle of the umbrella into the neck of the bottle (I assume that you have made sure that the umbrella fits). Then lay the bottle on the cord and you will see how the bottle and umbrella keep their balance just like genuine tightrope walkers!

48. The merry roundabout

You will need: bottle, cork, needle, aluminium plate, 2 corks, 4 forks.

Slice the corks down the middle and stick a fork into each slice. The fork must not be exactly at right angles to the cork, but at slightly less than 90°, or else the forks will not stay hanging from the plate. Put a cork in the neck of the bottle and push a needle into the cork. After having carefully found its exact centre you can balance the plate on the point of the needle. Very gently turn the plate round, let go and, since the friction is very small indeed, the plate can continue spinning for quite a considerable time.

49. Equilibrium — a kitchen still-life

You will need: plate, ladle, straining ladle, jug.

After a bit of trial and error you should succeed in achieving the set-up shown in the picture below. You must make sure beforehand that the end of the ladle grips the rim of the plate very firmly and that the ladle cannot slip over the plate. You can prevent any slipping by gripping a piece of cork or a wad of paper between the plate and the handle.

50. An acrobatic egg

You will need: bottle, egg, cork, 2 forks.

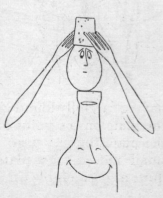

Hollow out a cork on the underside so that it fits exactly on the pointed end of an egg. Stick two forks into the cork and put it on top of the egg. Now put the egg on the edge of the neck of the bottle. After a little adjustment you can get another surprising example of equilibrium. If, however, you are not successful, the outcome will not be so surprising!

51. Make a seesaw from a candle

You will need: long candle, long nail, 2 wine glasses, 2 saucers.

From a candle you can make a seesaw which will continue to rock for quite a long time all by itself. To be able to do this the candle will have to burn at both ends. Scrape away some wax from the flat end so that the wick is exposed. By balancing the candle on a narrow edge of some sort, or on a knife, you can find exactly where the middle is. Push the long nail through the candle at this point. Rest the nail on two wine or water glasses. Now you have a seesaw, but how can you make it rock? Light the wicks at both ends; from one end of the candle a drop of molten wax falls, and that end rises because it is a little lighter. A bit later, a drop falls from the other end of the candle, and so it goes on. The balance of the candle is always being upset, with the result that the candle continues to rock up and down.

You can make the seesaw more interesting by cutting two little figures out of tinplate. If they are joined by a long strip of the tinplate you can fasten them to the candle with two drawing pins in the middle. To prevent a mess on the table or tablecloth put a couple of saucers under the candle.

52. A double cone which rolls uphill

You will need: some thick paper, a pair of scissors, glue, a sticks, a large book and a small book.

That something should roll uphill is indeed highly unusual and is actually impossible, unless the thing has the necessary speed. What we are going to do now is not to make the impossible really possible, but to make the impossible seem to be possible.

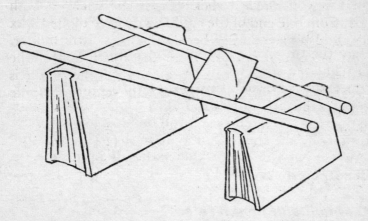

From thick paper or thin card make two cones which you then fasten together with glue or gummed tape. Put a large and a small book on the table with their backs upwards. On them lay two sticks or curtain rods with their upper ends further apart than their lower ends.

Now lay the cone close to the smaller book on the two rods and you will be surprised to see it run uphill along its 'rails'. The double cone rolls uphill!

But does it really go upwards? Look at the points of the cones. They go downwards, and so the cone itself really goes downwards. But it *looks* as if it has the greatest contempt for the law of gravity!

53. Make yourself a mystery box

You will need: ¾ yard of elastic, a short piece of string, a weight (e.g. a heavy nut), round tin (e.g. a syrup tin).

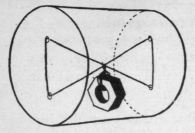

Yes, this tin which we are going to make is a really wonderful tin. In the lid and bottom bore two holes (two holes in each, of course). Thread a piece of elastic through the holes as you see in the drawing. Where the threads cross tie them together with a bit of string and then fasten on the heavy weight or nut. Now put the lid on the tin.

Lay the tin on the ground and push it away from you. The nut stays below the point of suspension and so the elastic gets wound up. Do not roll the tin too far, or the nut will start to turn round as well. Now let go of the tin, and you should see it roll back on its own, driven along by the energy stored up in the twisted elastic.

Anyone who does not know what is inside the tin will be quite amazed.

54. Pencil and penknife as balancing dancers

You will need: pencil, penknife.

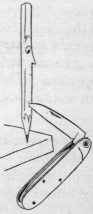

Open the penknife so that the blade makes a right angle with the handle and push the point of the knife into a well-sharpened pencil. Then let the pencil and knife balance on the edge of the table as shown in the picture. They have not the slightest inclination to lose their balance and it is possible to give the knife a gentle push, whereupon the whole thing rocks gently backwards and forwards.

As with all equilibrium experiments, this depends on the position of the Centre of Gravity and the point of support. By the Centre of Gravity of an object we mean an imaginary point at which the whole weight of the object seems to be concentrated. For a ball, for instance, the Centre of Gravity is at the centre. The Centre of Gravity of the pencil-penknife combination is low, maybe in the handle of the penknife, in any case lower than the point of support. Hence it cannot fall over.

55. An even more wonderful example of equilibrium

You will need: hammer, rule, piece of string.

If you hold an ordinary carpenter's rule on the edge of a table with the hinge below, the outer half naturally falls downwards. You can prevent this happening by hanging a hammer on it! It sounds unbelievable, doesn't it?

Hang the hammer on it with a piece of string as in the picture and not only does the rule straighten itself, but you can let go of it completely! By means of the string the hammer acts as a lever which is pushed up by the right half of the rule. The heavy end of the hammer makes the Centre of Gravity of the whole thing come underneath the table, below the point of suspension. The experiment can also be performed with a straight lath, as is shown in the picture.

56. An unusual way to cut through a pear

You will need: pear, thread of cotton or wool, 2 sharp knives, cup of water.

A ripe, not too hard, pear can be cut through in a very unusual manner. To do this hang the pear up as high as you can by a cotton or woollen thread. As low as possible underneath the pear hold a sharp knife, edge uppermost. Now hold a match beside the thread so that the thread catches fire and burns through, dropping the pear onto the knife. Thus the pear is cut neatly through the middle. You must, however, hold the knife on the exact spot so that the pear does not miss it.

You can find the exact position quite simply by holding the pear in a cup of water very carefully so that it does not swing and then taking the cup away. Drops of water fall vertically from the pear and show us the exact place to hold the knife.

This experiment can also be done with two crossed knives, each with its edge upwards. The cross must be on the line followed by the falling drops. The pear, following the law of gravity, is neatly quartered!

57. Make a switchback for water drops

You will need: strip of oiled paper or plastic, some books of different sizes, glass of water, teaspoon and saucer.

A strip of oiled paper or plastic, (completely smooth, without bumps or wrinkles) is laid, as in the drawing, over several books of different sizes.

Ordinary paper will do if you cover it with soot from a candle or paraffin flame. It will probably be necessary to hold the paper steady with pins. Now you have made a very neat switchback for water drops. Gently let a drop of water fall on the highest part of the switchback; it rolls down the first slope, because of its speed it rolls up the second slope, and so on up and down the whole switchback.

If you give somebody else a spoon you can organise exciting competitions.

Experiments on sound

Our world is full of sounds.

If we live in the town or in the country we hear sounds all day long: the singing of the birds, the neighing of horses, the roaring of motor cars and aeroplanes, talking, singing, laughing, or screaming of people, the sighing of the wind in the trees, the humming of bees, and the buzzing of flies . . . not a minute goes by without our hearing sounds.

All the noises are so different that we recognise most of them immediately without seeing who or what causes them. If we hear 'Cock-a-doodle-doo' somewhere, then it can only be a cockerel unless someone is playing a joke on us. 'Miaow' is a cat. If a blacksmith is at work, or a carpenter, and if they hammer or saw, our hearing enables us to distinguish them immediately.

Some noises sound high, such as the chirping of a grasshopper, others sound low, like the rolling of thunder. The thunder is an example of a loud noise, the sighing of the wind is a soft noise. We find some

60

sounds disagreeable; for example, the nasty buzzing of a gnat, the squealing brakes of a car, the screeching of an owl and the screaming of the dentist's drill. There are other sounds which we listen to with much greater pleasure: the singing of a nightingale, or a girl with a beautiful voice.

What would the world be like without sounds? Still and dead and dreary. But worst of all—we could not talk to each other!

58. How sounds are made

You will need: thin wooden lath, knife, table.

Press one end of the lath down on the table and let the rest of it project over the edge. Push the projecting end downwards and let go. Owing to the elasticity of the wood the free end of the lath goes up and down. We say that the free end 'vibrates'. As it vibrates we hear a sound. Hold the blade of a knife firmly on the table, press the handle down and then let it vibrate freely. You hear a sound.

If a bee is sitting still on a flower you cannot hear it. But as soon as it flies away, letting its wings vibrate extremely rapidly up and down, we hear it buzz—we hear it make a sound.

By hitting a drum the drumskin is pushed in. Because of its elasticity the skin flies outwards, inwards, outwards, and so on. In short, it vibrates and we hear a sound.

The noise of our speaking, whistling or singing is caused by something vibrating, in this case a pair of 'elastic' bands in the throat: the vocal cords. If you speak and hold your fingers against your voice box you can feel the vibrations quite strongly. By hundreds of other examples it could be shown that *all sounds occur because a vibrating object sets the air vibrating too.*

What causes the differences between sounds?

A bee and a gnat make different sounds. What is the cause of this difference? It is in the frequency or pitch of the sounds. A gnat has very much smaller wings than a bee: the wings of a gnat go up and down much more rapidly than a bee's—they vibrate faster. So we get a higher note. The faster a thing vibrates, the higher is the sound it makes.

59. The faster the vibrations, the higher the sound

You will need: long wooden lath, table.

The lath which you used in experiment 58 is pressed on the table again, and you let the free end vibrate. Now shorten the free end by pressing a longer portion against the table. Let the free end vibrate again. It vibrates faster than before and the sound you hear is a bit higher. The shorter you make the free end the faster it vibrates, and so the higher the note becomes.

60 The bigger the vibrations, the louder the note

You will need: wooden or cardboard box without a lid, elastic band.

Besides the difference in the pitch of sounds there can also be a difference in their strength. If you thump hard on a door with your fist you produce a much louder noise than if you tap on it with a finger. And fortunately the sound of your breathing is not as loud as the rumbling of thunder!

You can understand very easily how the difference in strength is caused by using a lidless wooden or cardboard box with an elastic band round it. Pull the band away from the box a little and then let it go. It vibrates through very short distances and so the sound is weak. But if you pull the rubber band a good inch upwards before letting it go, then it vibrates strongly and you hear a much louder sound. The pitch is the same in both cases, but in the second the *intensity* is much greater.

If someone, in turn, sings, whistles and plays on a violin a note of the same pitch and the same intensity, in each case the sound is different. It is different in timbre, or 'colour' and the instrument producing it is quite easily recognised.

What is the cause of the difference? If you sing a note of, say, 400 vibrations per second, then at the same time notes of 800, 1200, 1600, 2000, etc. vibrations are set up. The note of 400 vibrations per second is called the *fundamental*, the other notes of twice, three, four and five times the fundamental are the *overtones*. The strength and the number of the overtones are different for each musical instrument and for each voice. We cannot hear the overtones separately.

A violin has many strong overtones and they give it its warm, full tone. A whistle, on the other hand, has fewer of these overtones and as a result it sounds weaker—it gives a piercing note. So, the frequency of the vibrations fixes the pitch of the note, *the number and the strength of the overtones determine the quality of the note*.

61. A lion's roar out of a box!

You will need: box (of card, wood or tin), pencil, piece of string, some rosin.

Within the confines of this box you can imitate the roaring of a lion or the growling of a dog. In the side of the box make a hole and through it push a pencil to which a piece of string has been tied. The string must

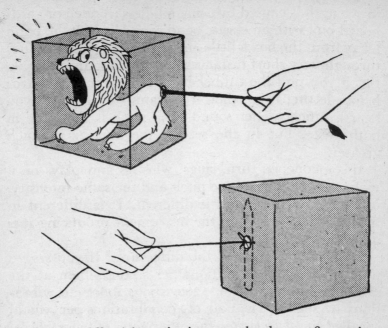

be made stiff with rosin just as the bow of a string instrument is.

Hold the box firmly with one hand, and pull along the string with the thumb and forefinger of the other hand. You will hear a loud noise which, depending on the box, is like the roaring of a lion or the growling of a dog.

Try this experiment also with other boxes of different shapes and different materials. The sound, which is caused by making the walls of the box vibrate, can be quite astounding!

62. Make yourself a 'rommelpot'

You will need: tin, straw several inches long, pig's bladder, piece of thin string.

In some parts of Holland boys go from door to door on Shrove Tuesday, singing songs and playing a 'rommelpot' and begging for pennies. A rommelpot like theirs is actually an expensive instrument, but it is well worth trying to make one for yourself. The deep growling which can be produced from a home-made rommelpot is almost as good as the powerful notes of a double bass.

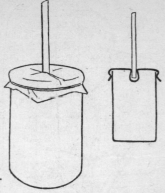

Let a clean pig's bladder stand in water for a few days and then fasten the middle of it to the end of a long, thin straw. Tie the string very tightly so that the straw is held quite securely. Stretch the bladder over the top of the tin, which should contain a little water. Make quite sure that the straw is exactly in the centre of the top of the tin. Pull the string very tightly before you fasten it off.

To play the rommelpot make your fingers damp— you can do it quite hygienically with water, though the boys in Brabant use their mouths as taps! The piece of straw must slide between your thumb on one side and the first and second fingers on the other. In this way you pull the bladder up and down and if you do it correctly you should hear the heavy growling that is characteristic of the rommelpot. With tins of different sizes you can get different pitches.

63. Hear the bells ring
You will need: thin string or thread, fork, knife, spoon.

It is quite easy to make a very effective carillon from ordinary cutlery. Hang a knife, a fork and a spoon on a string or thread as in the picture. Press the ends of the string against your ears with your fingers. Shake your head once or twice as though you were saying 'No'. The knife, fork, and spoon strike against each other and begin to vibrate. The vibrations are transmitted along the string to your ears, whereupon you find that the

sound is very like a loudly chiming carillon. Your carillon will sound purer if you get somebody to strike the metal objects with a pencil.

Of course you can enlarge the carillon with several more forks, spoons and knives of different sizes.

64. Make a telephone from old tins

You will need: 2 tins, long piece of string.

A telephone from old tins: and that is no April Fool joke! Instead of tins you could use waxed cartons like those that cream or ice cream are sold in.

Exactly in the middle of the bottom of each tin punch a small hole. Take about ten yards of thin string and put the ends through the bottoms of the tins. Knot the ends several times so that very large knots are made and the string cannot pull through the holes.

Because there is plenty of room out of doors take your tin-telephone outside. You hold your telephone—sorry, I mean your tin-telephone—against your ear and ask your friend to talk or sing into the other tin. The string must be fairly tightly stretched and must not touch anything. Even though the string is several yards long you can hear your friend's voice quite clearly.

The way the tin-telephone works is very simple. By speaking or singing your friend makes the bottom of his tin vibrate; the vibration is transmitted through the string and makes the bottom of your tin vibrate, and in turn the air near to it is made to vibrate.

65. How far away is the thunder?

You will need: 1 thunderstorm.

Sound is transmitted through the air at a speed of about 1,200 feet per second, while the speed of light is 186,000 miles per second. During a thunderstorm the flash of lightning is seen at practically the same time that it occurs. The sound of the thunder is heard rather later because the sound waves are transmitted so much more slowly than light. To find out how far away from us a thunderstorm is we need do nothing more than count the seconds which elapse between seeing the flash and hearing the thunder. If you haven't a watch with a seconds hand you can estimate seconds by counting slowly 'One-two-three-ONE, one-two-three-TWO, one-two-three-THREE' and so on. Then we divide the number of seconds by five and find the distance of the storm in miles.

66. Make a zither with elastic bands

You will need: cigar box (or a similar box of light wood), piece of three-ply or stout cardboard, some elastic bands.

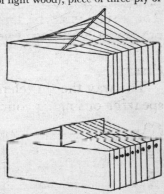

If you stretch a rubber band over a cigar box without a lid you can, by plucking, produce sounds of one note. That is rather monotonous, though. How about making an instrument on which you can play a tune? Cut a piece of three-ply or cardboard in the shape of a right-angled triangle and stick it upright on the bottom of the cigar box. In the sloping edge of the card make eight notches. Over the box and the 'comb' stretch eight rubber bands. With a bit of luck you can now play a scale.

Is it possible for the strings of your harp to be tuned? Yes—certainly. Now you must set to work to produce an arrangement as in the second sketch. For a 'comb' use a rectangular piece of three-ply. Into the side of the box carefully knock some thin nails and wind each band round the head of a nail whatever number of times you need in order to produce a scale. This 'tuning' can be done easily if you have a piano available.

67. Make a nail piano

You will need: some thin nails about 2″ long, large block of wood, small block of wood, hammer.

The drawing shows you how you can make a musical instrument from a fakir's bed. Drive nails into the larger wooden block so that each one is a little further in the wood than the one before it. Into the small block drive a nail also. With this nail tap the other nails and you get quite a pleasant ringing sound. By driving the nails further in, or pulling them out slightly, the instrument can be tuned to give a scale.

68. How to make a water trombone

You will need: milk bottle, glass tube, water.

This instrument is a very simple cross between a whistle and a trombone. Nearly fill a milk bottle with water. Put the glass tube into the water, pout your lips and blow across the top of it. If you do it the right way you will hear a note. The pitch of the note can be altered by moving the tube up and down in the water. The deeper it is in the water the higher is the note.

69. An organ from empty bottles

You will need: 8 milk bottles, vacuum cleaner (cylindrical type), water.

Naturally you must, at some time or other, have blown across the mouth of a bottle and produced a loud 'BOOM'. The bigger the bottle, the deeper the note. As you fill the bottle with water the note becomes higher according to the height of the water in the bottle. If now you blow across the mouth of the bottle you will produce a noise like a whistle. Do the same with the cap of your fountain pen and you get a piercing, strident note that can be heard two streets away!

Now try to obtain eight empty milk bottles. Stand them neatly in a row. Have some water handy in a jug, blow across the first bottle so that you produce a note and then pour enough water into the next bottle for it to produce the next note up the scale when you blow across it. For tuning your milk-bottle-organ you could use a piano or a mouth organ.

Now you ought to be able to play a tune on the organ by blowing across the different bottles, but it can

be very tiring. Therefore I suggest that you call in the aid of a vacuum cleaner. You will need one of the cylindrical type which can blow as well as suck. Put the pipe in the blowing end; you will not need the flat mouthpiece, just the plain open pipe. Switch the cleaner on and hold the end of the pipe at a slight angle by the mouth of one of the bottles. If you do it correctly you should hear a sound like the siren of a ship. Move the pipe along the different openings and different notes are produced. You can hold the pipe as far as two inches away from the bottles—then the note is loudest. Now try to play a tune starting with part of a scale, and carry on practising until you can play . . . well, I leave that to your own musical taste! After a bit of practice it is not difficult to play quite a good tune on your milk-bottle-organ. If you can get more bottles, say a pint and smaller, then you can increase the range of the organ considerably. It is an idea to stick on the bottles bits of paper with 'C', 'D', 'E', etc. If you can get sharps and flats you can make some real progress.

When you get bored with the organ you can convert it into a kind of xylophone without any difficulty by merely tapping on the bottles with the handle of a knife. But you will get quite different sounds and the fullest bottle will not give the highest note, but . . . the lowest note!

70. Wails from a ruler

You will need: flat ruler (or a strip of plywood with a hole in the end), piece of strong string.

Pull the end of the string through the hole and tie it tightly. Then whirl the ruler round on the end of the string very rapidly. You can do this in a number of ways: by letting the ruler whirl round on the string as you hold it in your hand, or by swinging your whole arm in a circle. By doing this the ruler, by spinning round very fast, produces the most amazing sounds, from a pleasant humming to the most heart-rending wails and roars. In amateur stage productions it is possible to use a ruler in this manner to imitate the howling of the wind or the roaring of a storm.

You can make a variation of this experiment by fastening the string to a stick which is whirled round rapidly. Or by using several rulers or plywood strips of different sizes together, a very wide variety of sounds can be produced.

71. Make a harmonica from wine glasses

You will need: a number of wineglasses, water.

In what some people are apt to call 'the good old days' you would see at fairs, in the streets or at the seaside a man with a long series of partly filled wine glasses (partly filled with water!) on which, by rubbing the rims lightly with the fingers, the most beautiful notes and tunes were made. It is definitely worth the trouble to try to make such a glass harmonica for yourself.

First you might learn how to play it. To do this take a wine glass with a thin stem, wet your fingertip (which must be absolutely free from grease: wash with soda or a detergent) and rub, pressing very lightly, round and round on the rim of the glass. At first it is a bit difficult to get a good harmonious note, but if you persevere with your efforts, and the glass has the required properties you will certainly succeed. It is important not to press too hard and to be sure that your finger is aways damp.

When you are more or less master of the technique of playing on one glass then you are ready to set up a whole row of wine glasses to make a scale. As with the other musical instruments which you have made, you can tune each glass with the help of a piano by pouring water into or out of the glass. The notes which you can make with such a glass harmonica are extraordinarily pure and lovely and can be likened to those of a musical box.

72. The wonder of resonance

You will need: 2 similar wine glasses, some water, a small piece of wire.

When you lay two violins beside each other and pluck the A string of one of them, the A string of the other one starts to vibrate and give out a sound. This 'sounding together' is called resonance. In everyday life you can observe this phenomenon in many ways. Stand a small glass on the piano and play the notes one after the other, then the glass vibrates strongly with a certain note. Put two similar empty milk bottles side by side and blow into one so that a note sounds, then the air column in the other bottle immediately starts to vibrate and give out a note. In small closed places like a bathroom you can notice this phenomenon of resonance by singing a series of low notes. One of the notes will sound much louder than the others—this 'reverberation' can also be observed in many other places.

A delightful experiment, based on resonance, is the following: two wine glasses, less than a quarter full, are placed a short distance from each other. Each glass is tapped and a note is heard. By pouring water into either you can make sure that each glass gives out exactly the same note. Over one glass a piece of thin wire is laid. With a wet finger rub the rim of the other glass as was done for the glass harmonica, so that it goes a note.

Then the first glass starts to vibrate by resonance and the wire begins to jump about on its rim in the most comical way.

73. Make a musical instrument from cardboard tubes

You will need: cardboard tubes, string, small hammer, 2 wooden laths.

From cardboard tubes, the containers in which drawings and charts are often sent, you can make another musical instrument. The easiest way to begin is with similar tubes of the same kind of cardboard, and of the same length and diameter. The tubes are hung one below the other by strings as shown in the picture. To make a scale the length of the top tube must be measured and the others must be in the following proportions to it: 1 : 8/9: 4/5: 3/4: 2/3: 3/5: 8/15: 1/2.

The little hammer with which the tubes are to be struck can be made from a cork with a pencil pushed into it. You can write the names of the notes on the tubes. After a few tries you will certainly be able to play some delightful tunes on your 'Tubeophone'.

74. Make a flat-iron guitar

You will need: flat-iron, steel wire, board, 2 sticks.

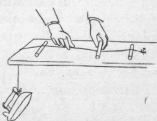

A comical instrument can be made by stretching a steel wire (from some other instrument) over two sticks on a plank. The stretching is done by fastening one end of the wire to a nail in the plank and hanging a flat-iron or other heavy article on the other end. With the third stick the length of the 'string' can be altered and, by plucking, notes of different pitches can be obtained.

Experiments on heat

If we take a piece of coal and split it in two, then split the half in two, and then split that half in two, we always get smaller pieces of coal. In the end we would get pieces so small that our chopper was too coarse an instrument to continue the dividing. No need to worry, we could carry on splitting the coal with a sharp knife. After a while we could replace the knife by the finest, sharpest and thinnest razor blade obtainable and, helped by a strong magnifying glass, we could go on for a considerable time splitting the coal into ever smaller halves. But in the end, even with the finest razor blade ever made, the fragments of coal would be so fine that further division was impracticable.

But just imagine that we could obtain a knife so fine and so sharp that it always kept keen enough for further dividing . . . then could we keep on indefinitely dividing the coal into ever smaller and smaller parts? Or is there a limit?

The answer is: Yes, there is a limit. If we could obtain a fragment of coal about twenty-five-millionth of an inch across we would find that it was indivisible. The Greek word for indivisible is *atmos*, from which we call the indivisible piece of coal an *atom of coal* or rather, an *atom of carbon*.

The scientists have been able to show that all that we see, all that is around us, and hence the people, the animals, the plants and the houses, the fields and the mountains, the seas and the clouds—in short, the earth and everything that is in it and on it—consist of innumerable atoms, the majority joined together in little groups called *molecules*.

Suppose that we have a piece of lead, a cube with sides about half an inch long. Such a piece contains about 30,000,000,000,000,000,000,000 lead atoms. These atoms do not lie closely packed together like the crystals in a bag of sugar. They all lie loose at a definite distance from each other.

At ordinary temperatures each atom has its own fixed position, but it does not remain still in this place. Each atom vibrates rapidly backwards and forwards.

Now what is the difference between a piece of lead that has been lying in ice water for some hours and a similar piece that has been in boiling water?

We cannot see a single difference between the cold and the hot piece of lead, but if we touch them we can feel that one piece is cold and the other is hot. What is the difference between hot and cold? It is in the movement of the atoms. The atoms vibrate back and forth all the time. Well now, the faster and stronger their movement, the hotter is the lead. If we heat a cold piece of lead, then the atoms vibrate much faster.

And, as you know, as it becomes very hot, lead melts. Now we are in a position to understand quite easily how this happens. The motion of the atoms becomes so vigorous that they no longer remain in the places where they vibrate to and fro, but move in all directions. This is the case with all fluids. In fluids the atoms or molecules move in all directions like ants in an anthill. But if we continue to heat the now liquid lead, it starts to boil and gives off lead vapour just as boiling water gives off water vapour. Now what do the atoms do?

This, too, is quite easy to understand. As a liquid boils the atoms move so rapidly that many of them no longer remain in the liquid but shoot out, up into the air, like winged insects that have been walking on the ground and then fly off. The boiling and evaporation of a liquid are therefore no more than the atoms or molecules gaining so much speed that they escape from the liquid and fly free—just like the atoms or molecules in a gas!

Oh, dear . . . the molecules are certainly moving fast today!

By cooling a substance, the speed and the movement of the atoms and molecules become steadily less and at a temperature of —273° Centigrade, the Absolute Zero, all the particles are still.

Whether a thing is warm or cold is therefore decided by the speed at which the atoms and molecules which make up the substance are moving.

75. Is the handkerchief fireproof?

You will need: handkerchief, 2 pence piece, lighted cigarette.

Hold the 2 pence piece under the handkerchief which you then pull tight round it. Make sure that the material lies very close to the surface of the coin. Now what will happen if you hold the lighted end of a cigarette against the cloth? Do you want to know? Well then, try it!

'Yes, but I am not going to risk my handkerchief,' you'll say. Still, you can try it quite safely, really; nothing will happen to your handkerchief. Without the coin you would burn a hole immediately (you can prove this with a bit of old rag), but with the 2 pence piece, or any other coin or flat piece of metal, it does not happen, because the metal conducts the heat away. The heat which the glowing end of the cigarette gives out is conducted away by the metal and not even a scorch mark is left on the handkerchief.

76. Boiling water in a . . . paper basin!

You will need: sheet of stiff paper, 4 paper clips, water, flame.

Don't you believe it is possible to boil water in a paper basin over a flame? You expect the paper to catch fire from the heat of the flame? Oh, come...

Nothing is more convincing than doing the experiment. From a piece of stiff paper make a small dish of the type shown in the picture. Fix the corners securely with paper clips. Then fill the paper dish with water and put it on the gas. Take care that the flame does not reach that part of the paper above the water, and that the corners are not in the flame.

After a while the water will start to boil without the paper getting burnt. During the heating the water takes away the heat which the paper receives from the flame, and the paper never gets hotter than 212° Fahrenheit, the boiling point of water. This temperature is very much lower than that at which paper catches fire.

If sometimes, when you are camping, your kettle springs a leak, you will be able to make shift perhaps with a paper dish. Who knows what tasty soup you will be able to make in it?

77. A flame that you can light twice

You will need: piece of metal gauze, candle, matches.

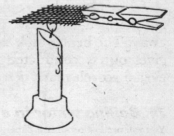

Light the candle and hold the gauze in the centre of the flame. Seeing that the gauze soon gets hot it is a good idea to hold it firmly with a clothes peg. You will notice that the flame does not burn above the gauze. That happens because the gauze conducts the heat of the flame away, and so gases and particles rising above the gauze no longer burn, unless. . . . Unless you hold a lighted match there! Then the flame burns quite calmly on both sides of the gauze.

(If you can get a piece of copper gauze, so much the better.)

78. Cold water is heavier than hot water

You will need: 2 milk bottles, hot water, cold water, ink, piece of waxed paper or thin card.

Put some red or blue ink in one bottle and fill it to the top with hot water. Fill the second bottle with cold water, lay the piece of waxed paper or thin card on top, hold it firmly and invert the bottle carefully so that no water falls out and put it gently on top of the bottle of hot, coloured water. Slowly pull the paper or card away and you will see the hot, coloured water rise like an elephant's trunk in the clear cold water. This happens because the warm water is lighter: it has a lower specific gravity than the cold water.

79. Feel the heat from your own head

You will need: reflector, head.

Heat is transferred by conduction—hold one end of a copper wire in a flame. By conduction the other end becomes so hot you may burn yourself. Heat is also transferred by radiation. The heat which reaches us from the sun is simply radiant heat. A light bulb also radiates heat. Hold your hand close to an electric light bulb of clear glass and switch on. The heat is felt instantly. But if you take hold of the glass bulb immediately after switching on you will notice that it is still cool.

Your body also radiates heat. In a cool room you can feel the radiant heat from your own body if you hold your hand or face in the right spot in front of a reflector. A suitable reflector would be one from a car headlamp, an electric radiator, a shaving mirror or a concave distorting mirror. You distinctly feel 'warmth' —the radiant heat from your own body.

80. The riddle of the sinking smoke

You will need: shoe box, candle, 2 lamp glasses, cigarette.

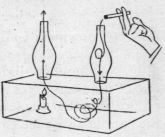

For most people it is not easy to obtain two lamp glasses of the kind that are used with oil lamps. You can manage just as well with two metal cylinders, e.g. round tins like kitchen powder tins with the top and bottom removed. But the experiment is just that bit more impressive with lamp glasses.

In the bottom of a shoe box make two holes, smaller than the diameter of the lamp glasses or tins. A candle and the two lamp glasses are then arranged as in the picture. The candle must be lit; take care that the shoe box is not set on fire. Now hold a cigarette over the right hand glass, and you see how the smoke goes downwards and rises out of the other chimney. How does that happen?

Warm air is lighter than cold air and so it rises. As a result the air above the candle goes upwards and comes out of the left hand chimney. But naturally air must be supplied from underneath. This air is provided through the right hand chimney and the force of suction is so great that the cigarette smoke is taken down with it!

81. A pair of scales for weighing air

You will need: candle, stick, some string, 2 similar paper bags, some adhesive tape.

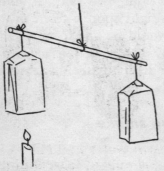

By means of the scales shown in the picture you can demonstrate very neatly that warm air is lighter than cold air. Hang a stick on a string. From the ends of the stick hang the two paper bags by means of short pieces of string and pieces of adhesive tape. The bags must have their openings downwards. By adjusting the string by which one of the bags hangs, make the stick balance horizontally. Now hold the lighted candle below the mouth of one of the bags—take care that you do not set the bag on fire!—and at the same time hold the bag still. Take the candle away, let go of the bag, and immediately it begins to rise. The warm air in this bag is lighter than the cold air in the other bag!

Experiments 15 and 16 in this book depend on the difference in density between cold and warm air.

Water experiments

82. Mothballs dance a ballet for you

You will need: glass or jam jar, some mothballs, some bicarbonate of soda.

If I were a moth I would certainly cheer if mothballs were not employed in any other way than that described on this page. And I would write enthusiastic articles about dancing mothballs for all the children's papers and books.

Fill a glass vase or tall jar with water and stir in a few spoonfuls of vinegar and a couple of teaspoonfuls of bicarbonate of soda. The stirring must be done very slowly or else it fizzes too much.

Into the fizzing liquid drop a few mothballs. At first they sink, but after a short time one mothball after another rises—right to the surface of the water—and sinks down again. But it does not stop there! It comes to the top again, sinks again, rises again, and so it goes on! All the balls dance slowly up and down—the mothballs' ballet.

How does it happen? Look carefully at the dancing balls. A ball has sunk. Then on its surface tiny bubbles of carbon dioxide collect; it is the same gas that you find in soda water and fizzy lemonade. Like tiny balloons they lift the mothball up. But when the ball reaches the surface so many bubbles escape into the air that the remaining bubbles cannot hold the ball up any longer, and it sinks. But down below new bubbles form on the ball and up it goes again!

The carbon dioxide bubbles come from the bicarbonate of soda and not from the mothballs. If the balls are too smooth the bubbles are unable to attach themselves. So make the balls rough with something sharp.

Hour after hour the mothballs go up and down and who knows . . . the moths themselves may come to look at this wonderful ballet.

83. Iron floats on water

You will need: bowl of water, needle, razor blade, piece of metal gauze.

Iron is about eight times as dense as water but even so it is possible to make iron float on water. Carefully lay a piece of gauze, a razor blade and a needle on some still water in a dish and you will see that the things stay floating on the surface. If you then touch the surface with a piece of soap they sink.

Perhaps sometimes you have seen pond skaters or other insects walking on the water. They do not fall through, any more than the iron things mentioned above do. This is because of the surface tension of the water. What that is, exactly, and how surface tension occurs, is a bit difficult to explain, but in practice it comes to this: that the surface of the water is very much like an elastic skin.

84. Make a boat propelled by soap

You will need: piece of card, sliver of soap, pan of water.

A piece of soap as a means of propulsion! How is that possible? By surface tension. But let us try it first. Make a little boat out of card; anything that looks like a boat will do. Cut a notch in the stern and fix a bit of soap into it. Put the boat in a basin of clean water, or into a full wash basin. The boat should move forwards. By fixing on a little rudder with a paper clip you can make your boat go round in circles.

The soap reduces the surface tension behind the boat and as a result it is pulled forwards. It cannot sail

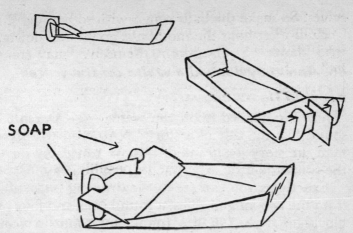

SOAP

for long on a bowl of water because the soap dissolves in the water and the tension is reduced over the whole surface. Then you can do nothing else but renew the water. The larger the water surface the longer the boat will sail. In a big pond it can easily keep going for an hour.

85. 'Repellent' soap and 'attractive' sugar

You will need: some matches, piece of soap, bowl of water, lump of sugar.

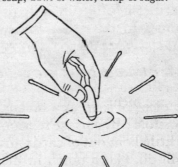

Lay the matches in a circle on the water and touch the water in the centre of them with a piece of soap. The matches are driven away so that they drift towards the edge of the bowl. If, however, you dip a lump of sugar in the centre the matches all come to the sugar. They obviously find the sugar very attractive. Because the sugar sucks up water a small current of water is directed towards the centre and so the matches are carried towards the middle. On the other hand, the soap exerts a similar action to that of the previous experiment, and the matches behave like children: sugar attracts them, but soap sends them away.

86. And they danced a waltz on the water

You will need: several corks, 2 long needles, some paper, piece of camphor, bowl of water.

'And they danced upon the water' . . . Doesn't that sound like the title of a story? Now, you will have to take the story for granted, but we can carry on with the romantic little experiment straight away.

Exactly as you can see in the drawing make a cross from the two long needles, a round cork and four small blocks of cork. On the round cork gum a pair of dancers cut from paper. It is essential to keep the whole thing as small as possible—the cross should not be more than 2" wide. Finally stick a small piece of camphor with balsa cement to the back of each of the

small blocks of cork. Now put the dancers on their cross on the water in the dish and, if all is well, the cross begins to turn round, the dancers begin to waltz in slow circles and the dance continues day and night for some time.

But . . . that happens only if everything is all right. What do we mean by 'all right' in this case? The experiment succeeds only if everything, including the cross and everything on it, the water and the bowl, is completely free from grease. The least trace of grease leads to failure. Therefore the greatest care must be taken in the making of the cross. First, the hands must be well washed, the bowl, too, must be well washed out with soda and hot water, and also the corks, the needles, and the water itself must be completely free from grease. If you want to be absolutely sure of the job then the complete cross and dish should be washed in ether. However, as this is a very dangerous liquid to have in the house, I think you should be quite all right if you use the hot water and soda. If all the grease is removed the dance can continue uninterrupted. So they waltz on the water, day after day . . .

87. From common egg to silver egg

You will need: hen's egg, glass jar full of water, candle.

Just as with every egg you take a few grains of salt to make it tasty, so you will have to take the 'silver' egg with a few grains of salt. There is no need to look for a Hallmark. This does not detract from the fact that the experiment with the silver egg is most attractive. Blacken a hen's egg (it could just as well be an ostrich's egg!) by holding it in the flame of a candle or over a smoky oil lamp. It then becomes covered all over with soot. Now lower the soot-blackened egg into a glass jar full of water and as soon as it is below the surface it takes on a glittering metallic shine—just as though it was silvered!

If you hold a silver spoon in a candle flame or smoky oil flame it becomes black. But hold it under water and it looks like silver again.

All articles which we make dead-black with soot, take on, under water, a shine as though they were made of noble metal.

88. A drop of oil propels a fish

You will need: basin of water, piece of paper, pair of scissors, drop of oil.

The picture alongside shows a fish drawn on paper. In the middle of it there is a circular opening which is connected by a "channel" to the tail. The fish is laid on water in a basin. The underside is in the water, but the upper side must remain quite dry. Now, very carefully, let a single drop of oil fall in the opening. The result is that the fish begins to move forwards. How does this happen?

The oil tries to spread out over the surface of the water. Oil always tries to do this and it is amazing what a large surface one drop of oil can cover. In still weather you can try this on a pond or ditch. As for the fish, the oil can only flow along the channel, that is, backwards. Oil is less dense than water and so it floats on top—and as a result, just as in a rocket or jet aeroplane, there is a force of reaction by which the fish moves forwards.

89. How to make a Cartesian diver

You will need: tall, narrow jar full of water, small bottle, hand.

The Cartesian diver, discovered by the great philosopher Descartes, used to be a favourite children's toy. It was often made in the form of a monstrous fish or demon. But this is now out of fashion in this age of plastics and flying saucers.

You can quite easily make a Cartesian diver for yourself. Fill a tall, narrow jar with water right to the top. Invert a small bottle in the water and let water into the bottle so that it will only just float. By 'just float' I mean 'not quite sink'! Make sure that the jar is absolutely full. Put the palm of your hand over the opening of the jar so that the jar is completely closed, then press down. The little bottle goes down—it sinks! Reduce the pressure, it comes up, press again and down it goes. In short your little diver dives most obediently on orders from your hand.

How is this possible? Air is easily compressible, water is not. The water is not compressed by your hand, but the air in the bottle is. The air occupies a smaller part of the volume of the bottle while the quantity of water in the bottle increases. Therefore the bottle does not float any more—it sinks. If the pressure is reduced, the air regains its original volume, and reduces the quantity of water in the bottle, which rises again.

If the glass jar is too wide for your hand to cover it entirely then you can lay a piece of plastic (e.g. a plastic jam pot cover) over it and tie it tightly with a piece of string. If this cover is airtight, then you can make the diver work by pressing on it.

90. Where does the salt go?

You will need: glass full of water, salt cellar full of salt, piece of thin wire.

The glass must be full of water, but not so full that the water is 'heaped'. Do you think that a tablespoonful of salt, which is quite a decent amount, can be put into the water without causing it to overflow? No, you probably won't believe it until—the old story—until you try it!

The salt, which must be well dried, is allowed to flow gradually out of the salt cellar while you stir with the thin wire. The volume of the water increases a little, but not anything like as much as you expected, in view of the amount in a tablespoon. It is more than likely that you can get the entire contents of the salt cellar into the glass without the water spilling over.

Certainly this is very strange. The volume of the water with the salt dissolved in it is less than the volume of the salt and the volume of the water together. Where does the salt go?

Water consists of water molecules, which—as in every liquid—are continually moving about, leaving quite large spaces between each other. There is then enough room between the molecules of water for the sodium atoms (in a solution the atoms of the solid are called ions) and the chlorine atoms (chlorine ions) of which the salt in solution consists.

91. Suspend an egg in water

You will need: large jam jar, water, egg, salt.

It is far from easy to suspend a thing in water. It happens only if the thing is exactly the same weight as the quantity of water which it displaces. But now, in order to suspend an egg in water we must make use of a trick. Salt water is heavier than an equal quantity of fresh water; we say that it has a greater specific gravity. An egg floats in very salt water and sinks in fresh water. We shall make use of this fact.

Half fill a jam jar with water in which a large amount of salt has been dissolved. If there is sufficient salt in the water, then, when we put the egg in it, it should float on the top. Now, very carefully and very slowly, pour fresh water down the side of the jar until it is almost full. Between the two liquids a boundary forms, but it is almost invisible to the naked eye. And the egg which sinks through the upper liquid floats on the lower liquid—the egg is suspended!

92. Your hand in the water – but it is not wet!

You will need: bowl of water, some lycopodium powder, coin.

Drop a coin into the water and ask your friends how it can be lifted out again without getting a wet hand. Rubber gloves must not be used. If you get some lycopodium powder from the chemist, by sprinkling some on the surface of the water it is possible to do what your friends confidently believe to be impossible. You can now safely put your hand into the water and take the coin out. And how surprised your friends will be when they see that your hand has remained completely dry.

But what is the explanation? As soon as you put your hand in the water it becomes covered with the powder, which possesses the remarkable property of not being 'wettable'. This occurs in other things too; think of a duck's feathers, which also remain completely dry even if they are completely submerged. The lycopodium powder surrounds the hand like a glove, a water-repellent, and so waterproof, glove. That is how your hand remains dry. If you cannot get lycopodium powder, talcum powder may work just as well.

93. Invert a glass of water without spilling it
You will need: glass of water, person with some daring.

Many of you may have seen in your childhood, on the beach, a bucketful of water being swung round on a string without a drop falling out. Though the bucket was upside down, the pull of gravity was counter-balanced by what is often called the centrifugal force, and so the water did not spill.

The trick is even more spectacular if an ordinary glass of water is used instead of a bucket. It is not quite so simple to swing the glass round without spilling the water. Therefore the glass must be held firmly in exactly the right way. Pick up the glass in the usual way but with the palm upside down. Then swing the out-stretched arm towards the right, upwards.

Take care that the movement is steady, not too fast but certainly not too slow. After a complete swing round take the position shown in the drawing and then the glass can be put on the table. It is worth advising you to make your first attempt out of doors or in the bathroom. . . .

Electrical experiments

The man leapt up as though electrified and asked, 'What is electricity?' 'That I will tell you,' said the other man, and he crept behind his typewriter.

Our bodies, the plants and animals, the earth and everything that surrounds us—all are built of countless atoms. But how can we picture these atoms?

Each atom is like a solar system in miniature, for rather as the earth and the other planets circle round the sun, so in the atoms the electrons circle round the nucleus of the atom.

So an atom is like a solar system in miniature, not 6,000 million miles across like the real solar system, but smaller than one 25-millionth of an inch. We ourselves also consists of countless multitudes of such systems. The tip of our nose contains thousands of millions.

Is it not a wonderful thought that we ourselves form a tiny universe? That the smallest vein, that the thinnest hair, that each blood corpuscle and lung air sac of the body, each and every one consists of millions of tiny solar systems, in which electrons revolve at high speeds round the neuclei of the atoms. That we are a mechanism of unpredictable, tiny, whirling wheels, that these wheels are so insignificant that all together they occupy only a thousand millionth part of us and we are practically as empty as the gigantic space in which the planets revolve round the sun at such great distances from each other. It is wonderful, but true. . . .

The tiniest particle of the body, and of everything else, bears the name *electron*, the Greek name for amber. This is no accident, for the old Greeks discovered, through amber, a natural force which, later on, was to be the power for the great source of modern industrial world—electricity. And between electricity and electrons there exist the closest ties.

For these ancient Greeks a small piece of amber was a delightful as well as a mysterious toy. They rubbed it on a piece of woollen cloth and held it over some little bits of dry leaves which then—flip!—jumped up and stuck to the amber.

I do the same but, as a substitute for amber, use my fountain pen which I rub on my pullover. An author has no shortage of pieces of paper and up! up! the pieces jump like tiny white butterflies attracted by this mysterious force. This force is called electricity, and it seizes these tiny paper butterflies without leaving a mark on them. Not a fingermark, but perhaps a faint trace—yes, who knows, a message from the under-world of the invisibly small; for electrons can leave microscopic traces.

Who or what gave me the idea to take my micro-scope, fix a piece of paper under the objective, peep through the eyepiece and adjust the focus? I don't know. But there I perceive a mysterious track of very fine, faint lines: the handwriting of the electrons. It is quite legible, and I read. . . .

May I introduce myself? My name is Electron and I am a representative of the Universal Electricity Authority. My firm supplies heat, light and power in any quantities that you may desire. It is not my intention really to sell you anything, or to make a very special offer. On the contrary my Directors have given me the honourable task of showing you the working methods of our company, a company which is able to undertake so much.

We, the electrons, employees in the service of the Universal Electricity Authority, are all holders of the world's lightweight championship. According to your methods of measurement a not inconsiderable total of about

10,000,000,000,000,000,000,000,000,000

of us weigh about 1 milligram—that is, about one four-hundred-thousandth of an ounce. We are the most insignificant beings in the universe and thus we have every reason to be modest. And yet, united in hosts of myriads, we are the driving force of everything that happens. If we should go on strike the stars would cease to shine and the entire universe would die down to a cold and motionless symbol of utter lifelessness. On earth we are less than slaves and mightier than kings, for as individuals we are nothing, united we are everything. And therefore, remember our motto: co-operation!

We, the electrons who are housed in the atom, are the bearers of negative electricity. There is also positive electricity, however, which resides in the atom nucleus. We are negative, the nucleus is positively charged; and the normal state of affairs is that the negative charge of all the electrons in the atom is equal to the positive charge of the nucleus. The result is that both kinds of charge cancel each other out and the atom is electrically neutral.

If this state of affairs is disturbed, however (for example, when some halfwit gets it into his head to rub his fountain pen against his pullover), a wholesale exodus of us electrons follows. We crawl out of the atoms of the wool on to the pen, and then the atoms in question are no longer neutral. The places we have come from have a shortage of electrons and so the positive charges of the nuclei are no longer cancelled out. The result is that the atoms become positive. On the place where we arrive there is a surplus, or excess, of electrons and so the atoms are negative. If we get the chance to return, then we stream in crowds from where there is a surplus to where there is a shortage of electrons, from negative to positive. This stream of us electrons is the electric current!

For preference we travel along well-made paths such as copper wire which offer us the least resistance and are good conductors for us. We have a dislike for materials such as glass and porcelain because they offer so much resistance that we cannot go through them. Such materials isolate (or insulate) us from the places where we want to go; so they are called insulators. But sometimes, if they try to resist us too much, we stand one behind the other in enormous numbers and, because we are now packed closely together, we can create enough pressure to force a way out for ourselves, making a great noise in the process. And this we do with such fiery enthusiasm that our break through is attended by a spark and a crack. Sometimes this develops into a noble display of power . . . a thunderstorm with lighting and thunder.

Generally we prefer to do it calmly and we travel along the beaten paths that have been prepared for us in the form of copper wires. As a rule we begin our journey in a gigantic reel of insulated copper wire which is driven round between the poles of a huge electro-magnet, in which other electrons induce a force which is called magnetism. All magnetism is our doing; and so the U.E.A. has a monopoly of this too.

As soon as we have left the coil with the magnet (the dynamo) we run smartly through the copper wire. On the way we meet a thin, little wire, made from the metal tungsten, inside an airless glass balloon. Then we press with so much force to try to get through it, and there is such a crush of us, that we bring the atoms of the little wire into violent motion which makes the wire white hot. Some of our electron colleagues make certain jumps and as a result the wire in the lamp gives out light. In some appliances the wire only becomes warm, e.g. in the electric cooker and the electric iron. As I have said already, the U.E.A. deals in light and power. We exert our force by means of a revolving coil of copper wire and with it we are able to deal with all sorts of jobs: motors, telegraphs, telephones, radios . . . their work is the work of us, the electrons.

Alas, my time and the space are limited. I had so much more that I wanted to tell you. How we feel as we throw ourselves into the maze of coils, resistances and condensers that is called radio. How all the different phenomena of light, the light of the glow-worm, a candle, a bulb, a discharge tube with which you are all familiar, are due to our jumps. (For light is caused by the jumps which we make from the outer paths round the nucleus to paths nearer the centre.) How all chemical actions, and also photography, are in fact our work. How by means of photo-electric cells we play detectives and can measure the light from distant stars. How we, as radio, can save men's lives, bridge oceans, guide aircraft and give pleasure and relaxation to hundreds of millions of people. How we can send moving pictures as television and how the most wonderful products of technology, from the radio valve to the electron microscope, are none other than our own workshops. But, as I have just said, my time and space are limited.

Let me end, therefore, by assuring you that we electrons still have a good deal in store for mankind. More than that, we hope that you will no longer misuse us for the stupidest and worst thing that men can do—wage war! But if you learn to co-operate as we electrons do, with a sincere regard for the welfare of your fellow men, then perhaps the day will come when we shall no longer need to sign ourselves:

Your humblest servant and your mightiest ruler,
Yours sincerely,
Electron.

I blinked my eyes, for I must have fallen asleep and had been dreaming of a pullover and a fountain pen; but I cannot recall it at all clearly. What really happened? Dreams are always fantasies—or are they?

But what was worse, I had slept and that meant a loss of time. And I had intended to deliver the manuscript quickly. But when my eye fell on the typewriter . . . again I blinked. For, you see, I do not believe in fairies, but I certainly believe in electrons and therefore. . . .

I must not dwell on it. I give you the letter from Electron as it has come to me, typed by a mysterious hand; and I introduce to you some experiments with electrons that you can do for yourself.

94. The comb and the ping-pong ball

You will need: comb, ping-pong ball, woollen cloth.

For the success of all the following experiments in static electricity it is essential that the weather should be dry. By dry weather I mean that the atmosphere should not be too damp. Experiments with static electricity are most successful in the winter in clear, freezing weather when there is a good fire burning.

Rub the comb briskly with the woollen cloth. In this way it becomes charged with electricity. Now bring the comb up to a ping-pong ball lying on the table. The ball is attracted by the charged comb and it rolls towards the comb. If you move the comb away from the ball, the ball rolls after it. It follows the comb as faithfully as a puppy.

95. The comb and the jet of water

You will need: comb, tap, woollen cloth.

Turn the tap on slightly so that a very thin stream of water comes out. Charge the comb with electricity by rubbing it with the woollen cloth and then bring the comb up to the thin stream of water. You will then see how the stream bends towards the comb, attracted by this magic force which we call electricity. Instead of a comb you could use a fountain pen or a rod of ebonite for all these experiments.

96. First attraction — then repulsion

You will need: comb, woollen cloth, some bits of paper, dry cork, pair of scissors.

With a sharp pair of scissors clip some fine shavings from a dry cork and hold a charged comb near a little heap of them. The comb is so attractive to the shavings that they jump up to it and stay there as though they had been stuck on. But it does not last long, for after a

little while most of the shavings jump off again. Why?

The negatively charged comb first attracts the uncharged, or neutral, cork shavings, but as soon as they get on the comb a share of the electric charge passes to them, so that they become negatively charged too.

Now, just as magnetic poles repel each other if they are alike, so do negatively charged particles repel each other. That is why the cork shavings hop off the comb.

Paper clippings too, and for that matter, any other small, light objects such as bits of fluff, peanut skins and fragments of ash, are attracted by a charged comb and are afterwards repelled.

97. High tension while you comb your hair

You will need: comb, head with hair, tap.

Have you ever, while you have been combing your hair in dry weather, heard a crackling noise? That was because you were generating a 'high tension'! On a dry winter's day you must try this again, but in near darkness. After you have combed briskly (or have rubbed the comb with a woollen cloth) hold the end of the comb about a quarter of an inch above a tap. They you will see a tiny spark jump across. In view of the fact that a spark measuring $\frac{1}{250}$ of an inch needs a tension of 200 volts it appears from the spark a quarter of an inch long that by combing the hair very high tensions can be generated—certainly more than 15,000 volts!

98. Give yourself a high tension of 10,000 volts

You will need: 4 strong glasses, piece of fur, tap, 2 people.

On a day that is cold and clear, and therefore dry, you can very simply give somebody a tension of several thousand volts without there being the slightest danger.

Dry the glasses thoroughly in the oven or in front of the fire and then stand them on the floor. Get somebody to stand on them. This person must stand quite clear of everything around him. He must not let his hands or arms touch the wall. Stroke him several times in succession on the back with the piece of fur and then get him to bring his finger near to the water tap. A spark will jump across.

There is absolutely no danger in it, and the electrified person feels no more than the very slightest pricking—that is all. And you will hardly be believed if you say that your assistant was standing there with a high tension of something like 10,000 volts.

99. Dolls dance by electricity

You will need: piece of glass, some thin paper, flannel or silk cloth, 2 books, pair of scissors.

In many stories you read 'The man leapt up as though electrified.' Well, now, we are going to make this a reality. From a very thin paper, such as cigarette paper, filter paper or tissue paper, cut a few pieces or some little dolls. In the drawing you can see examples of a man and a woman. Make each figure about an inch high. Now lay a piece of glass over two books which are a little thicker than the figures are tall. Lay the paper dolls under the glass and start to rub the glass with the flannel or silk cloth; then. . . .

Then the dolls jump up, electrified! For, by rubbing the glass you electrify it and it attracts the uncharged dolls so that they stand up. But when they touch the glass they also become charged and are repelled. So, down they lie again. The dolls lose their charge and the sheet of glass attracts them again. As long as you continue to rub, the dolls continue to jump up and lie down—they dance!

This experiment works best if you have the glass plate above an aluminium plate or lid so that the dolls, as they lie down, are in contact with the metal. A sheet of the aluminium foil which is sold for kitchen use is excellent for this.

100. An electric roundabout

You will need: glass, cork, pair of scissors, piece of paper, woollen cloth.

Cut from paper the pointed cross which is shown on the right of the drawing. Push a needle into a cork and on the point put the cross. Over both put a glass which has been well dried in the oven. With the woollen cloth rub a  part of the glass and the cross will turn round until the point stands opposite the place where you have rubbed.

Rub slowly with the cloth in the same direction round and round the glass and the cross will rotate. If you are fairly skilful at handling delicate things you can replace the cross by one with equal arms on which little paper horses can be hung by the thinnest of threads. Then you will have an electrically driven roundabout . . . with horses!

101. An electric ghost

You will need: 2 books, sheet of glass, cork, grater, paintbrush, some glycerine.

On the sheet of glass draw a doll, using the paint-brush and glycerine. Do it just as though you were painting a silhouette; that is, do not merely draw the outline, but fill in the whole picture with glycerine. Show the piece of glass with the 'unpainted' side to the front to your friends, and show it against the light.

Lay the glass over two books between which you have sprinkled some powdered cork. You can get powdered cork by rubbing the grater on an ordinary cork. Now rub the glass with the woollen cloth. The glass becomes charged with electricity and attracts the cork powder. Stop rubbing and some of the cork falls back on the table. Only the places which have been smeared with glycerine retain the cork. Lift up the sheet of glass, blow off the bits of cork which are still sticking to the unpainted parts of the glass and you are ready to show your friends the ghost produced by magic. You can probably project the shadow of your ghost on the wall with a lamp.

102. Electric soap-bubble ballet

You will need: fountain pen, woollen cloth, some soap bubbles.

If ever you blow bubbles on a winter's day you should try the effect of bringing a charged fountain pen or comb up to one as it floats in the air. The bubble is attracted. You can let bubbles fall on to soft woollen materials like flannel or doeskin. If you hold a charged comb over a bubble it is drawn upwards in a most comical way and takes on the shape of an egg. The attraction can, however, be so strong that the whole bubble is drawn upwards. By approaching different bubbles with the charged comb you can make them dance up and down quite merrily; the electric bubble ballet.

Instead of soap solution you can, of course, use a special liquid obtainable nowadays in small tins, with which very beautiful, strong bubbles can easily be made.

103. Electrical paper-hanging

You will need: sheet of thin paper, brush.

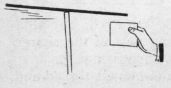

By rubbing a light sheet of paper with a brush or with your hand on a dry winter's day it can be charged with electricity. If it is then held up to the wall it will remain firmly 'pasted' there. The charged paper attracts the wall and because the attraction is mutual, the paper stays 'pasted' to the wall.

On the back of a chair lay a stick or rod so that it balances. Hold near one end of it a fairly tough piece of paper which has been charged by rubbing. Now you are able to make the stick fall without touching it. The stick is attracted by the electrified paper and then loses its balance.

The property that electrically charged things possess, of attracting other objects, is used in countering the nuisance caused by factory smoke. Through the chimneys millions of tons of soot and other particles escape every year, polluting the neighbourhood and causing the formation of fog. Moreover, vast quantities of valuable chemicals literally 'go up in smoke'. To prevent these things more and more factories are installing electrical devices to hold back the soot, dirt and chemicals. Electrically charged wires and plates are fitted in chimneys to attract the passing particles so that they can be reclaimed.

104. An electric pendulum

You will need: bottle with a cork, piece of wire, a silk thread, pocket comb, woollen cloth, 2 pith balls or pieces of cork.

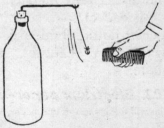

Dry the bottle in the oven, then push a piece of wire into cork and and bend it over. To the end of the wire fasten silk thread. Hang on the end of the thread a dried pith ball or a piece of dried cork. Bring the charged comb up to the pith ball and at first it will be attracted, but after touching the comb and receiving part of the charge from it, it will be repelled and it starts swinging.

If you hang on the wire yet another silk thread and

103

pith ball and then touch both the pith balls with the charged comb, they both receive the same kind of electric charge and repel each other—a very amusing sight.

105. Make yourself an electroscope

You will need: jam jar, aluminium plate, piece of copper wire, piece of thin metal foil.

An electroscope is a piece of apparatus for testing electric charges. You can make one of the simplest kinds by bending a piece of copper wire in the shape of a Z and hanging over the lower horizontal part a strip of thin metal foil folded double. Lay the upper horizontal part over the rim of a jam jar. Place an aluminium plate on top. A plain sheet of metal with rounded edges will do just as well. If you bring up to the plate a charged comb the strips of metal will repel each other—so long as everything is absolutely dry. Any electrically charged object brought near to the plate will make the metal leaves repel each other.

106. How to make a simple cell

You will need: small jam jar, piece of wood, 2 screws, 2 copper wires, plate of zinc, plate of copper, some dilute sulphuric acid.

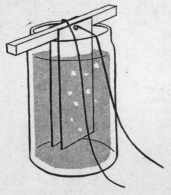

Screw the plate of zinc and the plate of copper to opposite sides of the piece of wood. Secure the ends of the two wires under the heads of the screws as is shown in the drawing. Make sure that the two screws do not touch each other inside the wood. Put the whole thing into a jam jar containing some dilute sulphuric acid. The acid can be obtained from a chemist, but be careful with it because it has a corrosive action. Now you have a simple cell, the distant ancestor of the flashlamp battery. With your cell it is unlikely that you will be able to light a bulb. But it will be obvious that electricity can be generated with this cell if you hold the ends of the two wires against your tongue. This causes a tingling feeling and a sour taste which shows the presence of the electric current.

107. A discovery that changed the world

You will need: simple cell, bowl of water, slice of cork, magnetised needle.

May I now invite you to try one of the most important experiments in the history of science? This is the experiment which was performed in 1820 by the Danish scientist Oersted, from which all applications of electro-magnetism, from the dynamo and the electric motor to telegraphy, telephony and the whole of modern electrical technology, have arisen.

In a bowl of water lay a magnetised needle on a slice of cork and let it rotate (see experiment 27). The needle will point north and south. Put the copper wires from your simple cell close above the floating needle and twist the ends together. Then you will see that the direction of the needle changes. Instead of your home-made cell you can use a torch battery. Then the wire through which the current flows can be at a greater distance from the basin, but the direction of the needle is still changed.

It is clear from this experiment that an electric current in the neighbourhood of a compass needle deflects the needle. A wire through which a current flows behaves like a magnet. The technical applications of this simple phenomenon have radically altered the whole aspect of our world.

108. Make an electromagnet

You will need: flashlamp battery, several yards of thin insulated copper wire, a bolt or nail 2½ to 4 inches long.

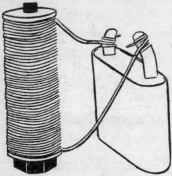

It is quite simple to make an electro-magnet. Round a bar of iron, e.g. a bolt or a large nail, wind several yards of insulated copper wire. Scrape the insulation from the ends of the wire for a distance of about three inches. Then wind one end of the wire round one of the brass strips which form the terminals of the battery. Hold the other bare end of wire against the other brass strip. Now bring the electromagnet near to some small iron objects such as nails and paper clips. You can see how they are attracted.

You can make your electromagnet stronger by putting on more turns of wire. To prevent the turns from sliding off it is a good idea to push two pieces of cardboard with holes in them over the iron rod, securing them with glue.

An even stronger electromagnet can be made by making two magnets from iron bolts and joining them together to make a large horseshoe magnet. Fasten the ends firmly by means of bolts into two holes in a strip of iron. If you have a disused electric bell or buzzer at your disposal you can get the electromagnet out of it.

It is quite good fun to fasten an electromagnet to a model crane and to insert a switch in the leads to the battery. When the current is switched on, the magnet on the crane can lift and hold quite heavy objects.

109. The magnetic field of a conductor

You will need: torch or cycle lamp battery, piece of copper wire, piece of cardboard, some iron filings.

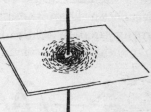

Push the wire through the cardboard and sprinkle some iron filings on the card. Connect the ends of the wire to the terminals of the battery and you will obtain the 'finger prints' of electromagnetism (see experiment 31) or, in other words, the magnetic field of a current flowing in a straight wire. The iron filings arrange themselves in circles.

110. Splitting cooking salt by electrolysis

You will need: glass, cycle lamp battery, 2 copper wires, water, some kitchen salt.

Put some water in a glass and dissolve a fair amount of cooking salt in it. Then hang in the solution two bare, uninsulated copper wires which you connect to the terminals of the battery. You will see that as long as the wires are connected to the battery, bubbles of gas come from the one connected to the negative terminal, while from the other a yellow-green substance descends. At the same time some heat is produced. Here we are dealing with the chemical effect of a current which, in this case, splits the dissolved cooking salt, or sodium chloride, into its elements: sodium and chlorine. The sodium unites with the water to make caustic soda and hydrogen. The latter you see as the rising bubbles of gas. The chlorine forms copper chloride with the copper which then reacts with the caustic soda to make copper hydroxide.

111. Iron filings create abstract patterns

You will need: battery, a few yards of copper wire, piece of cardboard, iron bolt, some iron filings.

By making a coil as in the drawing you can obtain an even more interesting and intricate field than in experiment 109. Along the axis of the coil lay the iron bolt, sprinkle iron filings on the cardboard and connect the ends of the coil to the terminals of the battery. You can keep the beautiful magnetic fields if you spray them with the fixative which you can get from art shops for preserving pastel drawings.

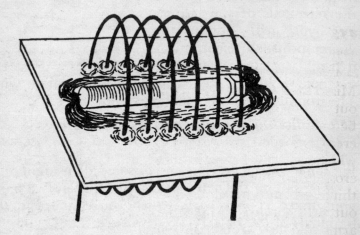

112. The mysterious portrait

You will need: 3 pieces of cardboard, piece of bell wire, battery, some gummed paper tape, iron filings.

On a piece of card draw a face, as in the figure, and cut away the card from round it. Cut the eye out too. Stick this piece of card to a larger one, oblong in shape. Now lay the bell wire carefully round it in such a way that it follows the outline of the face exactly. With glue or gummed tape fix the wire securely so that it does not come loose. Now lay the third piece of cardboard over the other two and secure it firmly with gummed tape.

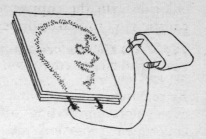

Sprinkle some iron filings over the card and connect the ends of the wire to the battery.

Then, as you tap gently on the card, the face appears as if by magic. If you make it all so that the wires and battery are invisible, and use a concealed switch for switching on the current, then your spectators will be quite astonished by this mysterious experiment!

113. Dance, Miss Paper Clip!

You will need: small wooden plank, small wooden block, wooden lath, piece of wire, rubber band, piece of paper, scissors, 8 paper clips, electromagnet, cardboard box, flashlamp battery, switch, some screws and nails.

Miss Paper Clip dances without a magnetiser having to be present! On a small board erect a wooden upright on to which you can fasten a bent crosswire. From stiff paper or thin card cut out a doll without arms or legs. Make the arms and legs from pairs of paper clips hooked together. When you have provided Miss Paper Clip with arms and legs hang her up on an elastic band. One inch beneath her put the strongest electromagnet that you can make and cover it with a cardboard box to make a dance floor. Put a switch in the leads to the battery, e.g. a push button such as is used for an electric bell.

By repeatedly pressing the switch the current, and thus the magnetism, is switched on and off. Miss Paper Clip is attracted in little jerks and by the elasticity of the rubber band and the liveliness of her arms and legs she dances very merrily. And so Miss Paper Clip on her electromagnetic dance floor is a wonderful child's toy.

Experiments with light

'*Light:* the natural agent that stimulates the sense of
sight; medium or condition of space in which
sight is possible; appearance of brightness.'

Concise Oxford Dictionary.

'I'm afraid you're pretty
dim, my boy. But this
cousin Albert of yours,
he really is a bright lad!'

What is light?

Light is a vibration phenomenon; it is an electromagnetic vibration and a wave motion. The only
difference between the waves of light and radio waves
is the wave length. Those of radio range from a few
inches to a few miles. The wave length of light waves
lies between 7 ten-thousandths of a millimetre (red
light) and 4 ten-thousandths of a millimetre (violet).
The total number of vibrations per second of red
light is:

$$400,000,000,000,000,000,000$$

What is the cause of light?

The electrons circle round the nucleus of the atom in
orbits of different diameters. Through certain causes
electrons jump from the inner orbits to the outer
orbits. From these the electrons jump back to the

inner orbits. That is how light is caused. All the light that we see originates from the jumping of the electrons from the inner orbits to the outer ones.

How fast is light?

The speed of propagation of light is 300,000 kilometres (about 186,000 miles) per second. The light from the moon reaches us in $1\frac{1}{4}$ seconds, the light from the sun covers the distance from the sun to the earth (93,000,000 miles) in about 8 minutes. But there are star systems which are so far away from us that their light, in spite of its tremendous speed, needs hundreds of millions of years to reach the earth.

Light travels in straight lines. We can see this if we set in line some cards each of which has a little hole in it. Behind the last card put a lamp, and look through the hole in the first one. You will find that you can only see the light if all the holes are in a straight line.

White light is a mixture of differently coloured lights. This becomes obvious if white light, e.g. sunlight, shines through a prism or the bevelled edge of a mirror. If the light then falls on a white wall we see on it the colours of the rainbow, red, orange, yellow, green, blue, indigo and violet. The mixture of all these colours produces white light. A prism, or the bevelled edge of a mirror, splits the mixture into its separate components.

An object is red if it reflects only red light. From white light (which is a mixture of different colours) falling on it, a red thing reflects only the red light and the other colours are absorbed. A yellow object reflects only yellow light, a white object reflects all the colours, a black one reflects no colours at all. We see the objects because of the light which they reflect.

'Father, what kind of berries are those?'
'Those are blackberries, my boy.'
'But, father, they are red!'
'That is because they are still green!'

114. Make a sodium light

You will need: saucer or tin lid, some borax, some methylated spirit, some coloured objects and pictures.

Put some lumps of borax on the saucer or tin lid and pour a little methylated spirit over them. Darken the room and light the meths. At first it burns with a blue flame, but before long a bright yellow light appears, sodium light, the same light that is given out by the sodium lamps that are used for road and street lighting.

If you look at a red object in the yellow sodium light it seems to be black. Look at a blue object and it, too, appears to be black. A green object—the same. What is the reason?

Of all the colours of light that are allowed to fall on a red object only the red is reflected. The other colours are absorbed. The sodium light contains nothing but yellow; there are no other colours mixed with it. But pure yellow light is not reflected by a red object, nor by a green object. Therefore we see everything black. But if you hold a white object in sodium light then you see it yellow, for a white object reflects all colours, including yellow. And a yellow thing? You see that yellow—it reflects yellow light, of course.

It is extremely interesting to look, in the light of your home-made sodium light or by the yellow street lighting, at all sorts of differently coloured objects and coloured plates from books and magazines. All colours, except yellow, seem to disappear completely. It is possible that red, blue and green seem to be alike and appear as dark grey or flat black. These remarkable changes are not so noticeable if the pictures are

113

viewed in the yellow light from a lantern or a lamp with a yellow glass, because then the yellow light contains several other coloured lights as well. With sodium light this is definitely not the case, and in it everything looks either yellow or black.

Sodium light is particularly suitable for use in street lighting because it is soft and pleasant to the eyes, yet the contrasts are sharpened. Another advantage is that the sodium lamp burns very economically.

115. Make a camera obscura

You will need: old tin without a lid, sheet of oiled, or waxed or greaseproof paper, elastic band, dark cloth.

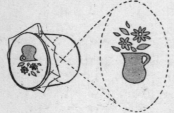

From a tin without a lid, for instance a large jam tin, you can make a small model of a *camera obscura*, the dark room which in former times was built sufficiently large for several people to sit in it and marvel at the landscape which, projected through a hole in the wall, was seen inverted on the opposite wall.

Over the open part of the tin stretch a piece of translucent paper, e.g. greaseproof paper, and secure it with an elastic band round the rim. Make a small hole in the centre of the bottom of the tin. Set up the tin in front of a window giving a view of another house, a street or a landscape well lit by the sun. Over your head and over the back end of the tin lay a large dark cloth or a blanket which does not let the light through. If you have your eyes about a foot from the paper you will see a picture of what there is outside, in natural colour, but smaller than life and . . . upside down! The drawing will show you why the picture is upside down.

The picture may not be very bright. It becomes brighter if you make the hole a little bigger, but it becomes less sharp. But if you put in the hole a small lens, you can get a picture which is both sharp and bright. You must arrange the lens and the paper so that the distance between them is the same as it would be if you were focusing the sun's rays on to the paper in order to set it on fire. By this means you obtain a camera obscura which is very much like a camera with a ground glass screen.

116. Red, green and blue light together make . . . white!

You will need: 3 torches, piece of red, piece of blue and piece of green 'Cellophane', sheet of white paper.

If you cannot get red, green or blue 'Cellophane', you can colour clear pieces in the required colours with inks or water colours.

Over each of the three torches stretch a different piece of coloured 'Cellophane'. If you now switch on the torches you will get a red, a green and a blue beam of light. What colour will you get if you let the red and the green lights fall on the white paper together? Quite a different colour from what you probably expected—yellow! And if you add the blue light to it, you get white! To get pure white you may find it necessary to hold the torches at different distances from the paper.

117. How to make a kaleidoscope

You will need: piece of mirror glass, glass cutter, piece of cardboard, some gummed tape, 2 elastic bands.

Of course you must, at some time, have folded a piece of paper over several times and then cut shapes out of it. When you opened out the paper 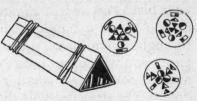 you got a sort of doyley in which the cutout shapes made a pretty, regular pattern repeated many times. You can make even more surprising patterns with a kaleidoscope. To make one you will need an old square or rectangular mirror or a piece of broken mirror that is big enough for two strips $1\frac{1}{2}$ inches by 7 inches to be cut from it. To do this you will need a glass cutter. If you have not got one, go to a shop where glass is sold and ask if someone will cut the glass for you.

From a piece of cardboard cut a strip the same size as one of your pieces of mirror. Paint one side of the cardboard black. Now lay the two pieces of mirror and the strip of cardboard (black side inwards) against each other in the way shown in the picture. Over the edges stick gummed tape and for safety put a couple of rubber bands round the whole thing.

If you look from above into the kaleidoscope at some coloured beads or pebbles, matches and other small objects laid on something flat underneath you will see, to your great surprise, delightful, many coloured, regular star-shaped designs. Rotate the kaleidoscope, then the patterns move and change continuously—just like a fairy story film in colour. With two or three matches, or a few small flowers or paper clips, you can make really beautiful patterns, because you always see six reflections in the mirrors.

If you cannot get silvered glass you can still make the kaleidoscope from ordinary glass. But how can the glass be made to reflect? By painting one side of it black. The black-painted side of the glass must be on the outside. Or you can stick black paper to the outside of the glass with a few drops of glue. In this way you can still get the mirror pictures, but they will not be quite as bright as those you get with real mirrors.

118. How to make a periscope

You will need: piece of cardboard $11\frac{1}{2}$ inches by 16 inches, 2 handbag mirrors 4 inches by 3 inches, gummed paper tape, pair of compasses, scissors, sharp knife, pencil, ruler.

If you are trying to watch a procession and there are

some very tall people standing in front of you, you can see nothing. If you want to be prepared against such a misfortune in the future make a periscope. Yes, a periscope just like those (of course, of a more elaborate pattern) which are used by submarines to see what is happening on the surface when they are many feet below it.

On a piece of card $11\frac{1}{2}$ inches by 16 inches draw three parallel lines, 3 inches, $2\frac{3}{4}$ inches and 3 inches from one of the long sides. (See the drawing.) Across the card draw a line $2\frac{3}{4}$ inches from the top. Cut out the piece marked X. The circle represents a hole in the card of about $1\frac{1}{2}$ inches diameter. It need not be an exact circle.

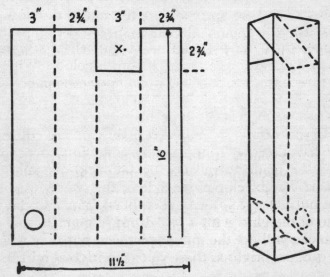

Fold the cardboard along the three pencil lines. You can do this best by scoring the lines with a sharp knife and folding the cardboard over the edge of a table. Then you will have a rectangular box like the drawing on the right. Now fix the two mirrors into the box with gummed paper tape. They must be fixed at angles of 45°, with the polished sides towards each other. When they are quite firm and the gum has dried you can close up the box with some more gummed tape. On the bottom fix a piece of card to form a good base, and on the top you can fix the piece which you cut out. And now you have a periscope ready for making your observations. You could sit at the window with it, with your head out of sight below the window sill, and still see all that is going on outside. Perhaps this offers some new ideas for playing hide and seek!

If your mirrors are smaller than 4 inches by 3 inches you will have to alter the sizes of the cardboard. If you have not heard of Pythagoras' Theorem you will have to make a little drawing like the one here and measure the side of the triangle. This will give you one dimension of the periscope. The width of your mirror will decide what the other side must measure.

119. Newton's rings

You will need: soap bubble, wet glass, piece of stiff white paper or card, candle or torch.

Of course you must, at some time or other, have seen the so called interference colours. The colours of a thin layer of oil on a puddle, the sheen of metals, the colours of mother-of-pearl and the colours of soap bubbles. What is the cause of them? They are not made from thin, coloured layers. The film of a soap bubble is quite colourless and is thinner than $\frac{1}{25,000}$ of an inch. That we see different colours is due to the fact that light waves of one particular wave length (and so of one particular colour of light) weaken or strengthen each other in the film, while waves of other wave lengths (and so of other colours) weaken or strengthen each other. This weakening or strengthen-

ing of light is known as interference; the colours which result from it are called interference colours.

With the aid of a large soap bubble you can observe these interference colours beautifully. Place on the table a piece of white card or paper (put it on a little stand so that it does not fall over), a wet glass and a lighted candle or torch. The distance from the candle or torch to the glass should be about 30 inches and from the glass to the white card about 4 inches. The room must be dark except for the light from the candle or the torch.

Now start blowing bubbles and try to get a large one to stay on top of the glass. On the screen you should see clearly the shadow of the bubble with coloured bands on it. These are Newton's rings. It is remarkable that these fairylike, beautiful rings do not remain in the same place all the time, but sink slowly towards the bottom, while from the top other colours continually start and slowly sink. If you blow very gently against the bubble there is an immediate distortion of the pattern and a change in the colours. Each colour that you see in a particular place depends on the thickness of the film at that place. We can imagine that a soap bubble consists of many very thin layers, one on top of the other. Each layer is about

119

$\frac{4}{2,500,000}$ of an inch thick. Where you see red there are about 150 layers, and where you see blue about 35. Instead of the wet glass you could use a damp glass plate, as you see in the picture, or try using a flat piece of dry flannel or woollen suit material.

120. Electric light from your arm

You will need: discharge lighting tube (possibly defective), arm.

The discharge tube has certainly come to stay, and no wonder, for it gives three times as much light as an ordinary bulb for the same consumption of electricity, and has a much longer life. In the tube there is mercury vapour which gives out mainly invisible ultra-violet rays. These rays fall on a powder spread over the inside of the tube and are converted into visible light.

You can make one of these tubes light without having to use the electricity supply. How? Simply by rubbing the tube rapidly, but not heavily, on an arm, preferably on a clear, dry winter's day. You must do it in a completely dark room! After a few seconds the lamp begins to glow, not with the usual bright light that you get when it is connected to the mains, but with a definitely visible white light. Where is the source of the power which supplies the energy for the light?

The power station is in your sleeve! When you rub the tube, electrons are drawn from the glass, which becomes positively charged and sets up a voltage. The resulting small currents cause the mysterious light.

121. Get the bird in the cage

You will need: small piece of card, thin string, pen or pencil.

Interesting though this little experiment is, it does not come up to the cinema or television. Therefore, in spite of its respectable old age, it has been almost forgotten.

Take a small piece of card and make two holes in it. Through each of the two holes thread a string. On the front of the card draw a cage, and on the back draw a bird. By twisting the strings very rapidly and making the card twirl round, you see in rapid succession, the pictures of the cage and the bird. Because of the slowness of the eye, which retains impressions of light for about $\frac{1}{16}$ of a second, you get the impression that the bird is not behind the cage but . . . in it!

Instead of a cage and a bird you can draw a basket with eggs (but then you must spin it carefully!), a monkey and a stick or a vase and flowers.

122. Joey, fly into your cage!

You will need: 2 pieces of white card, pen or pencil.

It is not necessary to go through all the instructions for experiment 121 to make the bird enter its cage; you can also make the bird do it itself. In the drawing you see the bird, and, about an inch away, the cage. On the dotted line stand a white card, the size of a  visiting card, at right angles to the paper, and hold the book in front of you so that the edge of the card touches your nose. Then you get the impression that the bird moves and enters the cage while you look straight at them.

You can draw similar pictures on cards for yourself, for example, the bird and the cage, or a bird and a man's head with wide-open mouth. Then you can make the bird fly into the mouth by first holding the card horizontally under your eyes and against your nose, then bringing the card with a quarter turn into the vertical, whereby the underside of the card remains touching your nose.

123. Let the wheels turn!

You will need: Book of Experiments, 2 eyes.

Rotate the book in small circles and you will be amazed to see all the wheels in the drawing going round, while the toothed wheel in the centre goes the opposite way!

Chemical experiments

124. A magic chemical garden

You will need: glass jar, copper sulphate, water glass, water, crystals of metallic salts.

Do you live in a flat? Do you long for your own garden? I cannot offer you that, but I can suggest something else— a magic chemical garden —under water! If you make it big enough you can wander round it in goggles and air pipe and do some gardening!

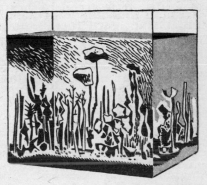

Into a large glass jar, e.g. a preserving jar, jam jar or an aquarium tank, pour a quantity of water glass, the stuff that is used for preserving eggs. Dilute it with three times as much water. Use distilled water if you can get it. For your 'seeds' you drop in some crystals of metal salts such as copper chloride, copper sulphate, copper nitrate, lead nitrate, manganese sulphate, aluminium sulphate, ferrous sulphate, ferrous chloride, nickel sulphate, and also some alum, some cobalt chloride and some cobalt nitrate. Many of these chemicals can be obtained from the chemist, but it is not necessary to use them all. A couple of crystals of each is quite sufficient. Crystals a little larger than $\frac{1}{8}$ of an inch across are the best. It is most important that the glass jar should be in a place free from vibration, e.g. a stone slab or a window sill. You can spread clean sand on the bottom of the jar to 'sow' your seeds in.

And now what happens? After a little while you will see all sorts of wonderful plant-like growths coming from the bottom of the jar, some with a very freakish appearance, in all sorts of different colours. Some look like algae, weeds and mosses. Hour by hour many more crystals grow like graceful corals and grasses which reach to the surface. The iron chloride crystals form brown branches; from manganese chloride and sulphate come icicles, copper and nickel sulphate give little blue-green bushes, and altogether you get a submarine garden of such exotic splendour that everyone who sees it will be quite amazed.

When the colourful fairy garden has grown, which takes several hours, let it stand undisturbed for a day. You must then siphon off the water-glass solution through a rubber tube and replace it by clean water. This must be done most carefully, so that the crystals are not broken. Then you will be able to keep your underwater garden for quite a long time.

125. A chemical imitation of a living cell

You will need: glass jar, copper sulphate, sulphuric acid, ammonium ferro-cyanide.

By chemical means it is possible to make something that has several properties in common with the living cell, the basis of all living things, which is visible only under a good microscope.

In a glass jar put 1 pint of water and dissolve in it $1\frac{1}{2}$ oz of copper sulphate (or $\frac{3}{4}$ oz in half a pint). Usually there is a milky precipitate which can be removed by adding a few drops of sulphuric acid to the solution. When the solution is clear drop in a crystal of ammonium ferrocyanide (which you can get from the chemist, though if you are under sixteen, you will probably have to have your parents' permission). On the surface of the crystal there then appears a film-like precipitate of copper ferrocyanide. By the process known as diffusion there is inside the skin an increase of pressure which makes the skin stretch and later split. Then the ferrocyanide comes into contact with the copper sulphate solution again and a new skin forms, closing up the hole once more.

This repeats itself over and over again, with the result that the cell keeps on growing until so much of the crystal has dissolved that the cell loses its 'vitality'. When it has all dissolved—and by this time the cell may well have reached a length of 4 inches—it loses the ability to close the little holes. Then it tears and slowly shrivels; eventually it falls apart in shreds—it dies.

Just like a living cell, this chemical reacts to stimuli from outside. Like a plant it grows upwards, even if the pot is stood at an angle. It also reacts to light, for in the dark it becomes grey, while in sunlight the growing point becomes green just like a germinating plant. Puncture the cell with a needle and the wound closes up immediately. And with some materials the growth of the 'plant' can be stopped. But you will have to investigate that for yourself.

126. From sugar to Pharaoh's serpent

You will need: ¼ oz of sugar, ⅛ oz potassium nitrate, ¼ oz potassium bichromate, some silver paper, 1 piece of card.

Chemists in every country in the world know what a Pharaoh's serpent is, but there is no reason why we should leave the delights of such snakes for the lords of chemistry to enjoy. Let us make one too. Three substances, ¼ oz of ordinary sugar, ⅛ oz of potassium nitrate, ¼ oz of potassium bichromate, must be separately ground fine and then well mixed together. Afterwards wrap the mixture in a piece of silver paper which is then put inside a small cardboard tube. If you light one end of your 'cartridge' a remarkable snake comes winding out of the tube and may grow many inches long.

127. Polish the silver

You will need: aluminium bowl, dish or plate, some baking powder, some cooking salt, a few silver articles.

The best and simplest way to clean silver is by electrolytic cleaning. Lay the silver in an aluminium bowl or dish, making sure that all the articles are in contact with the aluminium. Over the silver pour boiling water in which baking powder and cooking salt have been dissolved—one teaspoonful of each to a pint of water. The silver must be completely covered by the water. If you take the silver out after a few minutes, rinse, dry and then polish it with a soft cloth, you will see how brightly it shines.

Instead of salt and baking powder you can use a handful of washing soda.

A variety of experiments

128. Carbon dioxide is heavier than air

You will need: bottle, vinegar, some soda, wide glass bowl, 3 candles of different lengths, stiff paper, paste, round rod, scissors.

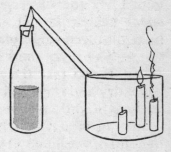

In the first place we must have a siphon for passing the carbon dioxide, which will be generated in the bottle, into the glass bowl. You can make the siphon for yourself by rolling some stiff paper round the rod and spreading paste on it, but not so that it sticks to the rod. Withdraw the rod and let the paper tube dry. When it is dry, cut it at an angle about three quarters of the way along and then glue the sloping ends together with strips of paper so that it looks like the tube in the drawing.

Pour vinegar into the bottle until it is almost half full and then drop some crystals of washing soda into it. Carbon dioxide gas is generated and rises in bubbles through the liquid. The short limb of the siphon is put into the bottle, and the long limb is propped up on the side of the wide glass bowl (e.g. a fruit bowl) in which the candles of different lengths are burning. Because the carbon dioxide is heavier than air it sinks down through the siphon and flows over the bottom of the bowl. Gradually the layer of gas becomes deeper. As it reaches the wick of the shortest candle the flame fades and eventually goes out. The other flames continue to burn peacefully, but they suffer the same fate as the layer of carbon dioxide becomes deeper, until all the lights in the bowl are extinguished.

129. Fire extinguishing with carbon dioxide

You will need: glass, some baking powder, vinegar, paper, candle.

There is an even easier method of putting out flames with carbon dioxide. Into a glass put half a teaspoonful of baking powder and pour on enough vinegar to half

fill the glass. Hold the glass at an angle so that the gas can flow along a gutter made of paper (see the picture) to the candle flame. The flame is soon put out by it.

Carbon dioxide is an important material for extinguishing fires. There

are fire extinguishers which project a dry powder which gives off carbon dioxide. You can demonstrate how they work by a small scale experiment. Make a tube of paper, fill it with baking powder and blow the contents suddenly into a metal bowl containing burning paper. If you do it the right way the fire goes out immediately, because of the formation of carbon dioxide from the baking powder, and because of the cooling effect of the baking powder itself. The carbon dioxide smothers the flames.

130. Glass rings from a broken bottle

You will need: bottle without a neck, some oil, poker, stove or fire.

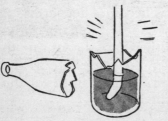

From a broken-necked bottle it is very easy to make a glass jar with a smooth rim, and also some glass rings. Fill the bottle with oil, for example, salad oil or gear oil, to the height at which you wish to cut it off. Make sure that the bottle stands absolutely level. Then hold a poker or iron bar in the fire or a gas flame until the end is red hot. With a rapid movement plunge the red hot iron into the oil. You will hear the glass crack, and you will notice that the crack is perfectly circular. Lift up the top piece of the bottle and you have a nice glass jar.

By pouring some of the oil out of the jar and once again plunging the red hot poker into it you get a second circular crack and a neat glass ring. It is especially interesting to try this experiment with a complete glass bottle and cut off a whole set of glass rings.

131. Cut glass with . . . scissors!

You will need: bowl of water, pair of scissors, piece of glass.

It is possible to cut glass with ordinary scissors in any shape you wish, provided that while cutting you hold the glass and the scissors as well as your hands completely under water. The water deadens the vibrations which make the glass crack. Yes, under water, glass can be cut almost as easily as cardboard.

132. Write with invisible ink

You will need: sheet of paper, pen, lemon.

In adventure stories you often read of old documents which indicate the site of a hidden treasure but which are written in cipher. With what excitement the attempts of the hero to decipher the instructions are followed! We are going to write a different kind of secret message, however— with invisible ink. . . .

When you use this 'invisible' ink you can see what you write; but as soon as it has dried the writing becomes invisible. When you send the letter to the person for whom it is intended you need have no fear that another person will be able to read it.

Your pot of invisible ink is . . . a lemon! So, cut a lemon in two. From one of the halves make a glass of tasty lemon squash, and dip a pen with a clean nib into the other. Push your pen firmly into the flesh of the lemon and make sure that the nib is thoroughly wetted by the lemon juice. Not too much, though, for otherwise you will make invisible blots!

And now, write with firm strokes so that the writing is not too thin. You get the best results with a pen which writes fairly thickly.

When you are at the end of your letter you may find that the beginning is already quite invisible because the lemon juice has dried. If you send the letter through the post it seems to me that it would not be very sensible to write the address in invisible ink as well!

How can the invisible ink be made visible again? By warming the sheet of paper very carefully, with the written side down, over a candle flame, a gas burner or a warm stove. Do take great care that the paper does not catch alight, otherwise the writing becomes invisible for good! While it is being heated the invisible writing becomes gradually brown—and visible. And so you can read the letter.

If you have no lemon handy, instead of lemon juice you can use vinegar. But lemon is much better.

A letter with nothing in it is a bit suspicious, don't you think? Do you know what you can do about that? On one side of the paper write with ordinary ink, but on the other side write your message with lemon juice.

133. Write with disappearing ink

You will need: some starch, cup, some water, iodine, paper, pen.

Stir into a cup of water some starch to which you have added a few drops of tincture of iodine. Make it into a thin paste. This is your ink. If you write with this ink you get dark brown writing. When the writing has dried, and you wipe it with a cloth or with your hand, it disappears without leaving a mark—and for good.

134. How to make picture candles

You will need: several candles, some printed pictures, matches.

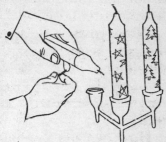

It is very simple to transfer to candles the printed pictures which are to be found in magazines and pamphlets. It works best with pictures printed on thin paper with strong black lines. Of course the pictures must not be wider than the circumference of a candle.

To transfer a picture to a candle, roll the paper round the candle with the printed side inwards, pressing it firmly against the candle. Now, slowly, but not too slowly, move a burning match along the underside of the paper—that is all. Strip the paper off and you will find that a black and white picture shows up in dark grey on the candle. It is also possible to transfer colours, provided that the coloured lines are strong enough. Generally this trick is more successful if the printing is fresh. You should certainly have a try at making picture candles, it is good fun and in any case the younger children will be delighted with the results. Perhaps at Christmas you can delight your visitors with candles on which you have printed all sorts of Christmas patterns.

135. Bore a hole in a halfpenny

You will need: halfpenny, needle, 2 blocks of wood, cork, hammer.

How can this be done? Very easily. Push a needle through a cork from end to end. The point may project a little, but the eye must not. If the eye does project a little, cut it off with a pair of pliers. Now lay the halfpenny on two blocks of wood, put the cork on top—the point of the needle downwards—and give a sharp blow on the cork with the hammer. Because steel is harder than bronze the needle goes through the coin.

136. How to make big soap bubbles

You will need: bowl of soapy water, wire, some sugar.

Form the wire into a ring by winding it once round a bottle and twisting the ends together. Dip the ring into some soapy water in which you have dissolved some sugar to make stronger bubbles. Withdraw the ring very carefully from the water and you will see that it is covered with a film of the soapy water. Now, hold the ring right in front of your mouth and blow steadily and gently against the centre of the film. You should see the film take on the shape of a bag and swell steadily all the while that you are blowing. At last the back part separates from the rest to form a very large bubble.

When you have acquired some skill at this and can make really big bubbles you should try another method. Put your closed hand into the water, and open the fingers slowly by bending them outwards, forming a ring by keeping the tips of thumb and first finger together. If you now take your hand carefully out of the water a film of soapy water remains across the ring. Now hold your hand in front of your mouth with the palm upwards and the little finger away from you, and blow into your hand. If you do this skilfully, by gentle and steady blowing you can make a really marvellous bubble.

137. How to make fireproof threads

You will need: piece of muslin, some thread, empty egg shell, bowl of hot water, salt.

Make some very strong brine by dissolving in a basin of warm water as much salt as you possibly can. In the brine lay two yards of thread and a piece of muslin. Take the thread and the muslin out, let them dry and then soak them again in the brine. Let them dry again, and repeat this soaking and drying several more times. Outwardly there is scarcely any change in the thread and the muslin.

With the muslin make a little hammock by tying the thread to the four corners. Soak the whole thing in the brine again, let it dry and repeat several times. Hang the hammock up by the threads. Lay the empty egg shell in the hammock and set it alight. Then, to your surprise you should see that, though hammock and threads burn, the egg remains hanging. The fibres, of which the hammock and threads consist, are burnt, but thanks to the salt the ash is strong enough to support the weight of the egg.

138. The mirror is broken – April fool!

You will need: mirror, thin piece of soap.

As April 1st comes round each year it is not easy to think of something new. May I help you with a joke that is so old that it has probably been completely forgotten? With the sharp edge of a thin piece of soap draw on a mirror a number of faint lines in a pat-

tern looking like a set of beautiful cracks. Then it really looks as though the mirror is cracked. But hold a damp cloth ready as you break the sad news. Maybe there are tears, and some strong remarks about the 'cracks', but they will disappear just as quickly as you wipe away the marks and shout 'April Fool!'

139. The enchanted needles

You will need: several moderate sized needles, a few threads of cotton, piece of wood.

If you try to throw a needle, like a dart, at a piece of wood about a yard away, you will rarely manage to make it stick in the wood. However much force you use, you still cannot do it. But success comes like magic if you thread a piece of cotton through the eye of the needle. Then every throw goes home. You can draw rings on your piece of wood, and try to aim your steel javelins at the bullseye.

Magic? Oh—science does not believe in magic. It is the trailing end of the thread that gives the needle the properties of an arrow and makes sure that the point hits the wood at right angles. Only then will the point penetrate the wood.

140. Drawing pins as midget tops

You will need: drawing pins, smooth table or floor.

If you have bought a box of drawing pins, then you have, so to speak, bought a box full of little tops, for a drawing pin can actually be a perfect top. But how do we set such a tiny thing going?

Hold your hand horizontally with the palm upwards, and grip the 'stem' of the drawing pin between finger and thumb. With a smart twist of the finger and thumb, in which the thumb jerks outwards, let the little top fall on the smooth table or floor. If you do this in the right way—it takes some practice to get the right jerk—the top will go on spinning for some time. The drawing pin must be absolutely upright and must have a sharp point. It is quite possible to set the pin spinning on a plate or saucer, and you will enjoy watching the rapid pirouettes of the tiny pin.

141. The trick of the broken match

You will need: bottle, match, sixpence, glass of water.

Bend the match in half without breaking it. Then lay it on a bottle and put a sixpence on top. Ask your family or friends who can see how to get the coin into the bottle without touching the bottle, the coin, or the match. Nobody can do it unless . . .

Unless he knows the trick. Then he dips his finger in the water and lets a few drops fall on the spot where the match is bent. This makes the fibres of the wood swell and the angle which the two halves of the match form slowly becomes bigger and bigger until . . . the coin falls in the bottle.

142. Feelings which fool us

You will need: group of cigarette smokers, piece of ice, knife.

Where there is a group of people most of whom have a burning cigarette in their hand or mouth, you can play a smart little trick which shows how unreliable our senses are. Without letting anyone see, make a point on a piece of ice with a knife. Dry it well, then press it firmly against the neck of one of your friends. He will be startled and perhaps angry because you, according to him, have held the burning end of a cigarette against his neck. Then it is your turn to be surprised and show him the piece of ice.

143. You have two noses

You will need: nose.

If you hold your first and second fingers crossed and then rub the tip of your nose with them you feel two noses. But if you then count, you will find you have only one! How on earth does that happen?

 If you rub your nose with your two fingers in their usual position you will feel only one nose. The sensory nerve on the left side of the tip of the middle finger and that on the right side of the tip of the first finger create in your brain the sensation of one nose. But by crossing the fingers the impressions of the left side of the top of the first finger and the right side of the middle finger are combined. This combination is so unusual for us that we accept these two sensations separately and feel two noses.

144. Raising the ice block

You will need: bowl of water, block of ice, short piece of string, some salt.

In a small bowl of water lay a block of ice and ask your friends if they can see how to lift the block out of the water, using only one hand. Make sure that the string is so short that it cannot be tied round the block.

There is only one way to get the block out of the water and fulfil the conditions. If your friends don't know the secret the block stays floating in the water until. . . . Until you make the end of the string thoroughly wet in the water, lay it over the ice block and sprinkle some salt over it. This makes some of the ice melt on the top of the block and so the end of the string lies in a little pool of water. But heat is necessary for the melting and it is taken from the surrounding ice and melted water. The result is that the water freezes again. The string is then frozen firmly to the block and it takes practically no effort to lift the block of ice out of the water on the end of the string.

145. Make a real steam roundabout

You will need: bottle, coin, fork, pin, 2 corks, some wire, 2 empty egg shells, cotton wool, methylated spirit.

Only the older readers, perhaps with some nostalgia, will remember the old-fashioned steam roundabout with its gay decoration and its puffing, panting steam engine. We cannot conjure up a genuine steam roundabout for our young readers, but we can certainly make something like it that will give you every bit as much enjoyment as, say, an up-to-the-minute toy helicopter.

The steam roundabout which you are going to make is a variation of the jet boat of experiment 36, for here you are also going to make use of blown eggs for jet engines. Two empty egg shells with a hole at one end are to be used. From thin iron or copper wire make two small baskets for the fuel, and two pairs of rings with a loop above which passes round the egg shells. Fasten these loops with separate wires to the forks.

Into the neck of the bottle push one of the corks until it is just under the rim. Lay a coin on the cork. Exactly in the centre of the other cork push a needle. Also, stick two forks into the cork. Use aluminium forks if you have them so that the whole thing is not too heavy. The angles which the forks make with the cork must be such that the whole thing remains in equilibrium, while the pin rests upright on the coin and the cork and forks rotate easily.

Fill each egg shell about a third full of water. By means of the rings and the loose wires fasten the egg shells onto the corks. Under each egg hang a wire basket and put into it a wad of cotton wool soaked in methylated spirit. Then light it. When the water boils a jet of steam escapes from the hole in each egg and our steam roundabout begins to spin round cheerfully, thanks to its jet engines—to the delight of young and old.

146. Make a tightrope walker
You will need: 2 corks, 5 thin wooden sticks, 2 forks, piece of wire.

Yes, now we are going to make a tightrope walker. You can use a cork for his head, or a small potato on which you can draw a funny face in ink. The head, and the cork which serves as the body, are fastened together with a little stick sharpened at each end. Two arms

and one leg consist of thin sticks bent in the middle. The second leg is formed of one stick which must not be bent, for your little figure has to stand on it. Make a notch in the bottom end of the straight leg, then it will fit better on the wire that you stretch across the room. In the body of your little figure stick the 'balancing organs'—two forks. Now stand him on the wire and he remains there balancing nicely. Blow against him from behind and he will move along the rope. If he moves a bit jerkily then you can help your tightrope walker by greasing the wire a bit, or stretching the wire slightly at an angle.

147. How is it done?

You will need: match, knife, fork, spoon, table.

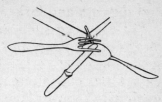

What you have to do is to lay a match on a table so that it overhangs the edge, and on the match hang a knife, fork and spoon—without making the match fall off.

Impossible? Well, try this way. Put the match on the edge of the table so that one end projects. Now clip the fork, knife and spoon together. For preference use a fork with four prongs which are not too far apart. Hold the fork in the left hand with the hollow side towards you. In the right hand take the spoon, also with the hollow side towards you. Next, clip the spoon between the third and fourth prongs of the fork. Between the back of the spoon and the fourth prong grip the blade of the knife. Now push one end of the match between the first and second prongs of the fork; the other end of the match remains on the edge of the table. With the match now well in the middle, carefully let go of the whole thing and then knife, fork and spoon remain hanging. Well, how *is* it done?

148. See your pulse

You will need: drawing pin, match, wrist.

You know the spot well on your wrist where you can feel how your heart pumps the blood through the arteries. The 'pulse' can be made visible by sticking a match on the head of a drawing pin which has a slightly rounded head. Balance the whole thing on the spot on your wrist where the beats feel the strongest. If you do this in the right way you will see the match move backwards and forwards with each heart beat.

149. Osmosis turns a small egg into a big egg

You will need: egg (e.g. a pullet's egg), bowl, some dilute hydrochloric acid, water.

Lay an ordinary egg for several minutes in a bowl with dilute hydrochloric acid. The action of the acid dissolves the shell of the egg, and you find that the white and the yolk are surrounded by a skin or membrane. By tilting the basin slightly pour the acid away carefully, then run plain water gently into the basin. You

must be careful here on two counts: you must be careful with the acid because it burns, and you must be careful to prevent the soft egg from breaking up.

Pour the water off again gently to make sure that all the acid is removed, then fill the basin with clean water a second time. You then see the egg swell up, and within 24 hours it has grown half as big again. And so the small egg becomes a big egg.

How does this come about? Osmosis. The skin of the egg contains very fine pores through which the tiny water molecules can pass but the large egg-white and protoplasm molecules cannot go. The water gets inside but the contents of the egg cannot get out. This phenomenon, which is called osmosis, happens in living things. By osmosis food solutions, and other things, can penetrate the cells of the human body without the protoplasm being able to escape through the separating walls.

The water has penetrated your egg, and has made the skin stretch. If you should replace the water in the dish with pure alcohol, which absorbs water rapidly, then you would draw water from the egg and it would regain its normal size. Replace the alcohol with water and the egg will swell again, and so you could go on.

150. Make an electric motor from nails

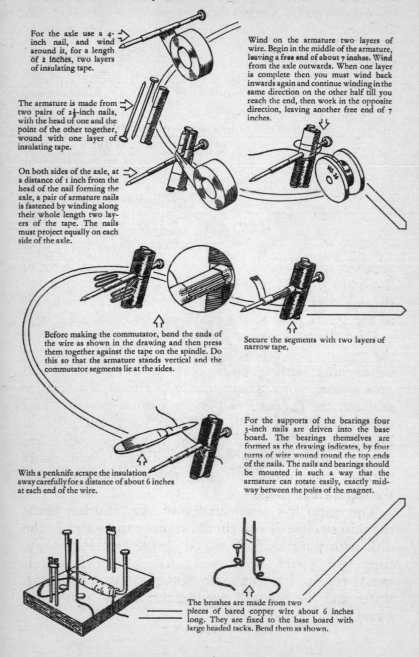

For the axle use a 4-inch nail, and wind around it, for a length of 2 inches, two layers of insulating tape.

The armature is made from two pairs of 2½-inch nails, with the head of one and the point of the other together, wound with one layer of insulating tape.

On both sides of the axle, at a distance of 1 inch from the head of the nail forming the axle, a pair of armature nails is fastened by winding along their whole length two layers of the tape. The nails must project equally on each side of the axle.

Wind on the armature two layers of wire. Begin in the middle of the armature, leaving a free end of about 7 inches. Wind from the axle outwards. When one layer is complete then you must wind back inwards again and continue winding in the same direction on the other half till you reach the end, then work in the opposite direction, leaving another free end of 7 inches.

Before making the commutator, bend the ends of the wire as shown in the drawing and then press them together against the tape on the spindle. Do this so that the armature stands vertical and the commutator segments lie at the sides.

Secure the segments with two layers of narrow tape.

With a penknife scrape the insulation away carefully for a distance of about 6 inches at each end of the wire.

For the supports of the bearings four 3-inch nails are driven into the base board. The bearings themselves are formed as the drawing indicates, by four turns of wire wound round the top ends of the nails. The nails and bearings should be mounted in such a way that the armature can rotate easily, exactly midway between the poles of the magnet.

The brushes are made from two pieces of bared copper wire about 6 inches long. They are fixed to the base board with large headed tacks. Bend them as shown.

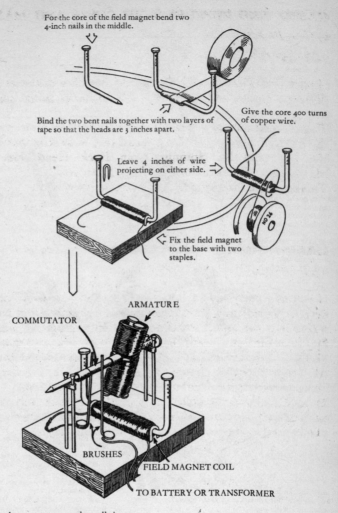

For the core of the field magnet bend two 4-inch nails in the middle.

Bind the two bent nails together with two layers of tape so that the heads are 3 inches apart.

Give the core 400 turns of copper wire.

Leave 4 inches of wire projecting on either side.

Fix the field magnet to the base with two staples.

ARMATURE

COMMUTATOR

BRUSHES

FIELD MAGNET COIL

TO BATTERY OR TRANSFORMER

Connect the motor to two dry cells in series (e.g. a cycle lamp battery), or better, a toy transformer of 6-8 volts. The exact position and pressure of the brushes must be found by experiment. The motor must not be switched off for long but should be kept with the current on.

YOU WILL NEED

30 yards of insulated copper wire (26 S.W.G.)
3 yards of narrow plastic or insulating tape
3 nails 4 inches long
4 nails 2½ inches long
2 staples
2 tintacks
1 piece of wood.

GAMES AND PUZZLES WITH COINS AND MATCHES

by Gyles Brandreth   40p

0 552 54102 8

Games and Puzzles with Coins and Matches contains over 80 different games and puzzles – all of them using coins and matches.

There are games and puzzles you can play on your own, and there are games and puzzles you can play with other people.

You can play The Spinning Coin Trick; Head Over Heels; Matchtaker; Spillikins; or Terrifying Triangles.

This book will bring you hours of fun and enjoyment.

MAKING MODEL AEROPLANES *by Peter Fairhurst*   45p

0 552 54099 4

If you had been alive a hundred years ago you would probably never have ridden a bicycle, you would certainly never have had a ride in a car and if someone had told you that he wanted to fly like a bird you would have thought he was a dreamer with his head in the clouds but his feet firmly planted on the ground.

All this was soon to change. In 1903 the Wright brothers made four powered flights. Man could at last fly like the birds.

Making Model Aeroplanes shows you how to make some of these early planes like the *Antoinette VII* and *Bleriot XI* as well as aeroplanes used in the Second World War like the *Spitfire*.

If you would like to receive a newsletter telling you about our new children's books, fill in the coupon with your name and address and send it to:

**Gillian Osband,
Transworld Publishers Ltd,
Century House,
61-63, Uxbridge Road,
London, W.5.**

_____

NAME ....

ADDRESS ....

....

....

CHILDREN'S NEWSLETTER